TABLE OF CONTENTS

ISBN 978-0-9749341-3-6

CREDITS:
Mary Kellogg-Joslyn and John Joslyn,
Cedar Bay Entertainment LLC, whose passion
made the *Titanic* Musuem dream come true.

Titanic Collectors, for their generosity in sharing
their treasures with the rest of the world:

Stan and Laurel Lehrer, Karen and
Ed Kamuda, Craig A. Sopin, Steve Santini
and Vera Hermanns, Edwin Davison,
Peter Davies-Garner, and Lewis Orchard

Missouri Life:
– Andrew Clay Barton: Design and
  Photography
– Ron Marr: Author
– Danita Allen Wood: Editing
– Greg Wood: Publisher

Relive the Past

Nestled in the trees of the Ozark Mountains, just 10 miles south of Branson, Missouri, is Big Cedar Lodge. Known in the 1920's as Big Cedar Hollow, home to Jude Simmons, business entrepreneur, and Harry Worman, Frisco Railroad executive.

In 1958, the White River was dammed to form Table Rock Lake and the stage was set for the Ozarks' premier wilderness resort. Following Bass Pro Shops' acquisition of the property in 1987, founder John L. Morris chose to restore the Simmons and Worman homesteads to their original prominence, initiating a rigorous commitment to renew the natural beauty of Big Cedar Hollow.

As you become a part of the Big Cedar Lodge family, the extravagant pages of our past will mingle with the more recent awareness of our environment to surround you in warm Ozark's hospitality. Whether fishing on Table Rock Lake, horseback riding, pampering yourself at the spa, golfing at Top of the Rock Golf Course or re-discovering natural beauty at Dogwood Canyon Nature Park, you'll find there is something for everyone.

Dorothy Worman

Harry Worman
Railroad Philanthropist

Constructed in 1921, the Worman Homestead was the original home of Harry and Dorothy Worman.

Stay in your own Private Log Cabin.

A glimpse of Valley View Lodge located at Big Cedar Lodge.

BIG CEDAR®
The Ozarks' Premier Wilderness Resort
Est. 1921

612 Devil's Pool Road · Ridgedale, MO 65739
(417) 335-2777 · www.bigcedar.com

To purchase a Big Cedar Lodge history book, please visit us online at www.bigcedar.com.

VACATION PLANNERS ARE AVAILABLE TO ASSIST YOU FROM 7:00 AM - 11:00 PM

As a young boy growing up in Wisconsin, I first encountered RMS *Titanic* when I read *Sea Disasters*, a collection of stories published by Columbia House Book Club. Each page filled me with wonder and amazement as *Titanic's* life-and-death struggle unfolded. Little did I know this book — this ship — would one day shape my destiny.

That day dawned in 1987 as I prepared to co-lead a six-million-dollar expedition to the wreck site some two years after *Titanic's* incredible, joint discovery by the Woods Hole Oceanographic Institute and the French exploratory agency, Ifemer. Our team's mission was to explore the wreckage, retrieve artifacts, and bring back film footage of the broken ship. These priceless images were shared with millions of people when "Return to the *Titanic* ... Live" aired in October 1987. I co-produced this television special with Doug Llewelyn after returning from the dive. With the help of an exceptionally talented crew, this *Titanic* special was the second-highest rated syndicated show of its time, something I still have pride and delight in today.

Titanic's discovery sparked the imagination of people around the world. As this grand, ill-fated ship experienced a rebirth, a new generation fell under her spell. At the same time, my dream of creating a permanent *Titanic* museum attraction began to take shape. Twenty years later, the World's Largest *Titanic* Museum Attraction opened in April 2006 in Branson, Missouri.

From the beginning, I knew *Titanic's* story was timeless and would be told and retold for generations to come. Unfortunately, myth and mystery attached themselves to her legacy over the years, making it difficult to separate fact from fiction. I was determined — obsessed, really — to get it right. After my emotional visit to the decaying hulk of that once-magnificent ship, I felt obligated to honor the people who faced death that cold April night in 1912. I knew then that their true stories of courage, sacrifice, and survival were the real building blocks of an enduring *Titanic* tribute.

Having a dream and making it come true would take more encouragement and support than I could have imagined. Fortunately, I discovered there are hundreds of knowledgeable people around the world — scholars, collectors, artists, and writers whose lives, like mine, had been touched by *Titanic*. In building *Titanic* Branson, I had invaluable assistance from this esteemed, international "family," and I am grateful to each and every one who helped make this man's impossible dream come true.

John Josyln and
Mary Kellogg-Joslyn

First, my deepest thanks to Robert Fleming, principal of Idletime Network, Inc. and probably the most creative individual I've ever worked with. From day one, he wanted to design the museum attraction in the shape of *Titanic*. He worked miracles, and his master touch is evident throughout the exhibit.

Building credits and thanks also go to Frank Turner and his construction company for keeping us on track, on time, and on budget. We could not have completed this project without him and his team.

One of Frank's team, Doug Bartlett and his own company, Theme Structures, Inc., deserves a special thank you. He shaped the ship and wrapped it in steel. Doug and his team worked around the clock to meet deadlines and their own high standards of quality.

Special thanks to Stanley Lehrer, founder and former president, publisher, and editorial director of *USA Today*. He is also recognized as a foremost collector of *Titanic* artifacts and memorabilia, collecting for more than thirty-five years. The wealth of his contribution and that of his wife, Laurel, is beyond measure.

Many thanks, too, to Edward Kamuda, founder of the *Titanic* Historical Society, for his great generosity, in

Initial drawings
by Robert Fleming

word and deed. Much of today's information about *Titanic* exists through the efforts and dedication of Ed. We are privileged to display many of Ed and Karen's artifacts.

Craig A. Sopin, legal practitioner and lecturer by trade, is by heart a *Titanic* aficionado and another *Titanic* Branson blessing. We are forever grateful to Craig for sharing his deep knowledge of *Titanic* memorabilia and collectibles and for opening his artifact collection to us.

To our Canadian friends, Steve Santini and wife Vera Hermanns, we say *merci*. Their input, enthusiasm, participation, and priceless pieces give our museum attraction its rich, historical perspective.

If it weren't for Edwin Davison, one of Ireland's own photographers and guardian of the priceless Father Browne *Titanic* photographic collection, the world would have lost the only film record of what life aboard *Titanic* was actually like. We are indebted to Edwin for making many of these incredible images available to us for display.

Our sincere thanks and gratitude go to Peter Davies-Garner of England for shaping the dream on a grand, imaginative scale. His incredibly detailed *Titanic* eighteen-foot model fills our first gallery with wonder and awe.

If I could, I'd tap a thank you on the authentic, 1912 wireless equipment to Felicia and Jim Kreuzer. Without them and their priceless wireless collection, a very special element in the *Titanic* story would be missing.

When Phillip Gowan came into our lives, we didn't suspect he'd soon become a major contributor to *Titanic* Branson's success. As one of the foremost historians of *Titanic's* passengers and crew, Phillip knows just about everything about everybody who was onboard. We can't thank him enough for sharing this information and for shedding new light on passengers' lives, hopes, and dreams.

Nobody has done more to preserve and perpetuate *Titanic's* epic story than James Cameron. His movie, *TITANIC,* breathed new life into this oft-told tale. We are proud to display the dramatic, twenty-six-foot model used in the film's opening sequence.

My associate in our Florida *Titanic* attraction, Paul Burns, introduced me to Robert Fleming, suggesting the two of us would make a good team. How right he was. Thank you also, Paul, for running the Florida exhibit.

Finally, a word or two about the most important person in my life and the life of the World's Largest *Titanic* Museum Attraction, my wife and partner, Mary. Without her none of this would have happened. Her enthusiasm for the project, coolness under fire, her organizational skills, creative talent, and resourcefulness were and are amazing to me. Twenty years as an executive vice president with the Walt Disney Company prepared her for the job at hand, but I was not prepared to watch her in action. The indomitable spirit of this woman, her keen eye and great heart quickly became the defining spirit of the whole place. She was the commander in chief of daily operations from day one, and I salute and thank her for all she has done to fulfill this dream of ours.

Others I'd like to acknowledge and thank include: Steve and Raeanne Presley for paving our way to Branson; Ken Marschall for his *Titanic* paintings; Lewis Orchard; Lee W. Merideth; Bruce Caplin; Lowell Lytle; Randy Bryan Bigham; Jeanne Waters and her team from Touché; the architect firm of Marshall, Waters & Woody (especially Ed Waters and Steve Guilliams); John Miller, Gayle Babcock, Lois Warner, and Jim Collier. The talents and resources of these individuals have helped shape *Titanic* Branson's legacy.

There are so many more friends, contributors and supporters who should be recognized. This has been a rich and rewarding experience, and Mary and I thank you all for taking this incredible journey with us.

Branson

You'd never guess one place could be so much fun!

To request your Vacation Guide,
please call 1-800-504-9339 or go to explorebranson.com

BRANSON
Lakes Area Chamber of Commerce and C...

WELCOME ABOARD!

THE MOST ACCURATE MODEL OF *TITANIC* EVER BUILT

There are few who know the secrets of the Royal Mail Ship *Titanic* better than Englishman Peter Davies-Garner. Though the pride of the White Star Line now sleeps in a watery grave two miles beneath the surface of the frigid North Atlantic, the talented hands of this world-renowned model-ship builder reveal the once-hidden details of the doomed liner in magnificent intimacy.

Construction of the eighteen-foot, 1:48 scale model of the *Titanic* took place in Germany and required two years of painstaking craftsmanship. Using copies of surviving remnants of the original *Titanic* blueprints created by shipwrights Harland and Wolff, as well as early photographs of the *Olympic,* the *Titanic*'s nearly identical sister ship, Davies-Garner's efforts resulted in what historians around the globe have called the most

Details such as hand-drawn deck seams and tiny rivets bring the model to life.

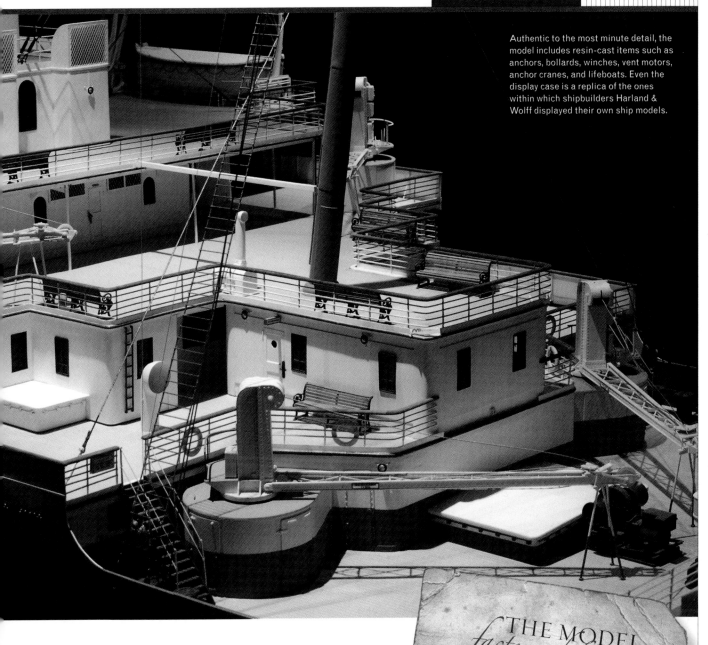

Authentic to the most minute detail, the model includes resin-cast items such as anchors, bollards, winches, vent motors, anchor cranes, and lifeboats. Even the display case is a replica of the ones within which shipbuilders Harland & Wolff displayed their own ship models.

accurate representation of the *Titanic* ever constructed.

A true labor of love, the reproduction includes touches virtually invisible to the casual observer. A closer look, however, will reveal that beauty can blossom in the smallest of venues. The decks of the *Titanic* model were created from maple veneer with deck seams drawn by hand. Deck beams, ceiling lamps, drinking fountains, and even doorknobs were added to bring the model to life both in the mind of the artist and in the eye of the viewer. In the hull are ninety-six thousand tiny rivets, all installed by hand.

This is the *Titanic* as she was in her glory, from imposing superstructure and lifeboats to private promenades, from anchors to capstans.

Through the skill of Peter Davies-Garner, the legend lives on.

THE MODEL
facts and figures

- ✗ 18 FEET LONG
- ✗ 1:48 SCALE
- ✗ 2 YEARS TO MAKE
- ✗ 96,000 RIVETS
- ✗ BUILT IN GERMANY BY AN ENGLISHMAN
- ✗ THE LARGEST ACCURATE MODEL IN THE WORLD

A NOTE FROM THE MODEL BUILDER

For me, it was a once-in-a-lifetime opportunity, and I was adamant in getting the completed model as close to the real ship as possible. I already owned copies of the Harland & Wolff plans, however, many of the original plans are lost and so some parts of the ship are left undocumented. In trying to fill in the gaps, one can safely rely on early photographs of the *Titanic*'s nearly identical sister ship, the *Olympic*, as both ships were built from the same plans.

In 1996, while I was still at the University, I started drawing my own set of *Titanic* plans, and I learned a lot about the ship and its structure in those days. These plans set the path for building this model. It was fun, frustrating, tiring, exciting, challenging, educating, at times even boring (the riveting).

One of the most daunting tasks was the shell plating and riveting of the hull. The story goes that it took three million rivets to build the real *Titanic*. It took ninety-six thousand to build this model; sixty-four thousand of these are in the hull. Only the round-headed rivets were included, as the flush rivets in the lower part of the hull weren't visible after the hull had been painted. Using the Harland & Wolff shell-plating and rivet-pattern plans, I was able to recreate every shell plate accurately and also push in every round-headed rivet precisely where it should be.

Looking at the model, I can say that it was all well worth it. I hope you enjoy it. — *Peter Davies-Garner*

THE MOST LUXURIOUS SHIP IN THE WORLD

The *Titanic* was the largest, tallest, and most luxurious ship in the world as she began her voyage, as well as the most worldly. She was built by Harland & Wolff at their dry dock at Belfast, Ireland; managed by the British White Star Line, whose original home port was Liverpool, England; and owned by the International Mercantile Marine, one of wealthy American financier J.P. Morgan's trusts. Morgan was scheduled on the maiden voyage, and in fact, his luggage had been loaded. Fortunately for him, business in Europe detained him. This model at the *Titanic* Museum at Branson is the largest in the world of the models considered accurate. Also in this gallery, you hear the somber reflections of survivors as well as final proclamations of many who died.

The Life of Riley

Employees of the Harland and Wolff Shipyard clocked in at 7:50 AM and clocked out at 5:30 PM. They were permitted a ten-minute break at 10 AM and a half-hour lunch, but no breaks in the afternoon. Saturdays were also work days, with hours from 7:50 AM to 12:30 PM. Although holidays were never paid, employees received two days off at Christmas, two days off at Easter, and a one-week break during the summer. These were considered exceptionally fair and equitable working conditions in the early 1900s.

Marconi Operator
Harold Bride
Survived

"...was taken down ... could not ... up ... I felt
myself whirled around, swam under water,
fearful that the hot water that came up
from the boilers might boil me up."

Passenger
Colonel Archibald Gracie
Survived

This photograph taken in May 1911 shows *Titanic*'s port side reciprocating engine nearing completion. Soon the engine would be dismantled and rebuilt in the engine room at the fitting-out wharf, shown in the photograph at right. There are nine photographs showing the great ship being built at the *Titanic* Museum at Branson.

THE SHIPYARD

THE NEW WHITE STAR LINER "TITANIC" 45,000 TONS NEARING COMPLETION.
DOCKED IN THE LARGEST GRAVING DOCK IN THE WORLD. BELFAST, FEBRUARY 1912.

THE BUILDING OF THE BIGGEST SHIP IN THE WORLD

More than a hundred thousand strong, they stood near the docks, their eyes glittering with justifiable pride and a tangible sense of awe as the great ship towered high above. It was a thing of magic, a thing of dreams. There was nervous laughter in the crowd, an indecipherable babble of voices. Small children climbed the wide shoulders of their fathers for a better look, the men pointing out the keel, the imposing funnels, the crow's nest, and always, the three million rivets, which had been pounded red-hot through the steel plating of the hull.

Nearly fourteen thousand workers who were amongst the crowd had assisted in the creation of the *Titanic*. They had worked long hours at the Belfast shipyard of Harland and Wolff, helping to give birth to

BEFORE SHE SAILED

This wood plane and clevis were used by shipyard worker Thomas McCauley to build the ship. In addition, the *Titanic* Museum also has his ball-peen hammer, keyhole saw, miter saw (also known as a backsaw), two wood planes, and a scribe. Today, the unknown workers who used tools like these would be considered master craftsmen. *(Titanic Concepts Inc. Collection)* This postcard was mailed on February 1912 from Southampton by Officer Herbert Pitman, a six-year White Star Line employee who would serve as third officer. He wrote on the back, "*Titanic* is the largest ship in the world," a distinction that no doubt brought pride to all of the builders and workers scheduled to sail on her maiden voyage. *(Stan Lehrer Collection)*

the greatest ocean liner the world had ever known. It had been dangerous work, and more than a few of their fellows had suffered injury. At least five young men died during the three years of seemingly endless, often tedious, labor. Still, on launch day, the men gazed at *Titanic* as if she were the Eighth Wonder of the World. They knew in their hearts they had come together to fashion something greater than themselves, something wondrous, something remarkable.

Unbelievably, they had shaped reality from a dream. Men such as shipyard worker Thomas McCauley recalled the filigrees and scrolls they had sculpted with simple hammers, keyhole saws, scribes, and wood planes. Others, like thirty-nine-year-old Thomas Andrews, no doubt felt themselves first-hand witnesses to the dawning of the future. Thomas, managing director of the design department of Harland and Wolff, had joined the renowned firm at age sixteen. Through brains, enthusiasm, and hard work, he had risen through the ranks.

On April 11, 1912, Thomas would board *Titanic* as a first-class passenger and, never one to shirk duty, spend much of his time composing notes, jotting down observations, and assisting the crew with minor difficulties that arose. On the frigid morning of April 15, he would be summoned to the bridge of the *Titanic* by Captain Edward J. Smith. Until then unaware that the hull had been pierced by an iceberg, the designer would undertake a quick survey of the damage and judge the ship doomed.

But on launch day, the tragic events of the future were still hidden within the mists of time. To the onlookers, the future seemed nothing other than bright.

The streets of Belfast witnessed the groans and screams of wood against steel as *Titanic* slid down the 772-foot ramp toward the harbor. Cushioned on twenty-two tons of soap and tallow, she made her way toward the water. The seconds seemed like hours, but in fact, the bow of the *Titanic* reached the water in just a little more than a minute. The date was May 31, 1911. The time was 12:31 PM. The circumstances that would lead to an appointment with tragedy had been set in motion.

To say that the construction of the *Titanic* had been a massive endeavor would be a vast understatement. She was 882.5 feet in length (three inches longer than her sister ship, the *Olympic*) and 92.5 feet wide. She displaced 66,000 tons of water and could travel at a top speed of 24 knots (nearly 28 miles per hour, or 44.4 kilometers per hour). The *Titanic*'s

Just before departure, *Titanic*'s firemen and engine-room workers would quench their thirst at a real spit-and-sawdust pub. A fireman who survived the wreck, John Podesta, described the visit: "Most of the firemen and trimmers go ashore again until sailing time. Having plenty of time, we dropped into another pub called the Grapes, meeting several more shipmates inside." This sign came from the actual 1912 Grapes, which still operates on Oxford Street in Southampton today. This is how the front looks today. *(Craig Sopin Collection)*

The photographer doctored the negative to show the dimensions of the starboard propeller shaft and to better balance the image, thus creating a ghost worker — and much speculation.

This scale model built by James Kellogg portrays accurately the rudder and triple-screw propellers. The *Titanic*'s stern frame stood 67½ feet high and weighed 70 tons. The rudder, more than 68 feet high, weighed more than 101¼ tons. The three gigantic propellers were of the highest quality, solid magnesium and bronze. *(Titanic Historical Society)*

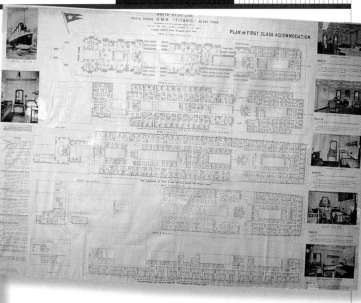

Tugboats assist the *Titanic* as she embarks from Belfast, Ireland. *(Stan Lehrer Collection)*

RARE ARTIFACTS

This First Class Accommodations Plan, issued March 29, 1912, is one of only three known to exist. All first-class passengers received copies to help them find their way around. The richly crafted, hand-carved wood panel below graced the *Olympic*'s first-class staircase, but similar decorations were aboard the *Titanic*. *(Both artifacts: Stan Lehrer Collection)*

stern frame stood 67.5 feet high and weighed 70 tons. The rudder, over 68 feet high, weighed 101.25 tons. The three gigantic propellers were of the highest quality, solid magnesium and bronze. The ship included 16 waterproof compartments and had capacity for 3,250 passengers.

Though the *Titanic* carried 3,560 life vests and 48 life rings, she was lacking in one vital item.

This oversight may have been born of arrogance, or perhaps it was simply overconfidence, a designer's sense of infallibility. The accolades for *Titanic* were arising from all quarters, and hubris may well have allowed both the White Star Line and her engineers to develop feelings of invulnerability. The White Star Line itself was promoting both the *Titanic* and the *Olympic* as "unsinkable," because of the watertight compartments that were supposed to seal against leaks or pierced hulls. It would not be the first time, nor the last, that improvement in technology led to an absence of simple wisdom and common sense.

The oversight, as the world would sadly learn too late, was that *Titanic* carried but twenty lifeboats.

Perhaps the hope and promise of the *Titanic*, and the catastrophe that would befall her, are best captured by Ken Marshall, the world's leading *Titanic* artist, in the more than one

hundred paintings he has made of the ship. The museum displays three of Ken's reproductions, including the one at right. As Ken himself describes the ship as inspiration, "So compelling and irresistible is *Titanic*'s real story ... Never has such a monumental achievement of human engineering and craftsmanship been created and lost so quickly. Never has there been a saga steeped in such superlatives, astonishing bad luck, drama, and heroism. ... It is a classic Greek tragedy, an exaggerated caricature, like a dream."

For those who steamed toward America, the sweet dream quickly descended into nightmare.

Back, from left: Purser Hugh Richard Walter McElroy, Second Officer Charles Herbert Lightoller, Third Officer Herbert John Pitman, Fourth Officer Joseph Groves Boxhall, Fifth Officer Harold Godfrey Lowe; Front, from left: Sixth Officer James Paul Moody, Chief Officer Henry Tingle Wilde, Captain Edward John Smith, First Officer William McMaster Murdoch

The Crew

Fourth Officer Joseph Boxhall, age twenty-eight, had assumed his bridge duty at 8 PM on the night of April 11, 1912. Hours later, while returning to his position after a short break, he heard the first warning bell from the crow's nest of the *Titanic*. Boxhall was the first of the crew to fire a distress rocket. In the early morning hours of April 12, he was put in charge of Lifeboat Number 2.

Twenty-nine-year-old Harold Lowe, Fifth Officer on the *Titanic*, did not awake until the *Titanic* was already listing at a severe angle. He immediately dressed, rushed to the boat deck, and began helping women and children to the lifeboats. Put in charge of Lifeboat Number 4, he was one of the few who rowed back into the mass of drowning humanity to search for survivors. He found four people in the freezing waters, all barely alive. Three of these four would live.

Artist Ken Marschall's paintings are known for their intricate detail and historical accuracy. This reproduction depicts *Titanic*'s departure from Queenstown, Ireland on April 11, 1912 at the poignant moment when she steams hopefully westward toward America yet into the setting sun. *(Courtesy of Ken Marschall; www.KenMarschall.com)*

THE BOILER ROOM

THE UNSEEN FIREMEN, TRIMMERS, AND GREASERS

The beating heart of the *Titanic* could be found in a place far removed from the sumptuous suites, elegant dining rooms, and pleasing promenades enjoyed by the upper crust of 1912's social registry. The boiler rooms were a world of heat, fire, steam, and smoke, an infernal region where men with arms of steel shoveled countless scoops of coal into the ravenous maws of 159 furnaces. In total, 5,892 tons of coal were laid in for the journey, as the insatiable furnaces required regular feedings to the tune of 630 tons per day.

Deep in the belly of the ship, more than three hundred men worked in shifts around the clock to assure that *Titanic* received ample power to slice the waves at a speed of up to twenty-four knots. Six boiler rooms contained twenty-four double-ended and five single-ended boilers, each containing six and three furnaces, respectively. Into the furnaces, the 177 firemen shoveled the mountains of coal, which were delivered to them by 73 trimmers, men whose vocation was to load and push ponderous wheelbarrows toward the sweltering boilers. Moments of rest were in short supply in the boiler room, both out of necessity and by design. At intervals of seven minutes, a gong would sound, and a number would appear on a dial, indicating which furnaces were most in need of stoking. There was no tolerance in the boiler room for the weak or the lazy.

Both the firemen and the trimmers were constantly covered by a thick veneer of coal dust. As a result of their dusky appearance, they were commonly known as "The Black Gang." However, if there was a

COAL SMOKE AND COAL DUST

Upper-class passengers lounged on deck chairs on private promenades, resting their eyes on the rolling whitecaps of the mighty Atlantic. But they did so beneath four behemoth smokestacks that belched smoke from the belly of the great ship. The firemen shoveling the coal stared only at ravenous flames, as they hoisted coal shovels that when fully loaded could weigh up to twenty pounds. The average person can manage no more than fifteen scoops per minute, for short periods of time. Imagine shoveling coal all day long. This postcard is one the White Star Line used in promotional materials.

TRY TO SHOVEL COAL INTO THE FURNACE

At the museum, visitors can feel the strain of scooping shovelfuls of heavy coal.

TEST YOUR KNOWLEDGE

HOW WAS *TITANIC* POWERED?

CONSTANTLY STOKED BY FIREMEN, *TITANIC'S* 159 COAL-FIRED FURNACES HEATED THE WATER IN 29 THREE-STORY BOILERS. THESE BOILERS GENERATED HIGH-PRESSURE STEAM THAT RAN TWO RECIPROCATING ENGINES, THUS TURNING THE TWO, MASSIVE OUTSIDE PROPELLERS. ANY LEFTOVER STEAM POWERED A TURBINE THAT TURNED *TITANIC'S* CENTER PROPELLER. THE STEAM THEN RAN THROUGH CONDENSERS THAT TURNED IT BACK TO WATER, AND PUMPS SENT THE CONDENSED WATER BACK TO THE BOILERS.

more loathsome job than fireman or trimmer, it likely belonged to the greasers. The onerous tasks of these twenty-four men consisted of crawling into cramped and scalding nooks and crannies to clean and lubricate the constantly filthy machinery. Greasers occupied the lower echelon of the boiler room's pecking order — a hard life. At the other end of the spectrum, a chief engineer oversaw the workings and proper operation of the boiler room, assisted by seven senior engineers and seventeen assistant engineers. There were also two boilermakers.

Life in the boiler room was an existence of which most passengers on the *Titanic* were largely unaware. After an elaborate evening meal in the first-class saloon on D-Deck, passengers would adjourn to the large, horseshoe-shaped reception room at the base of the grand staircase. There, the *Titanic's* band would perform light classical music and the latest hits of 1912 for the likes of the Astors, the Guggenheims, and a few lords and ladies from English society. Anyone who was anyone swayed, drink in hand, to the lilting rhythms of a beloved waltz. A few might attempt the new step known as the Foxtrot, still somewhat controversial in certain circles. As the night wore on, as a few inhibitions were shed, the band would launch into new forms of music, and the strains of "Oh, You Beautiful Doll" and "Alexander's Ragtime Band" complemented the perfume-scented air. Even in the steerage accommodations, the working-class passengers would keep step to the laughing tunes of a homemade fiddle, leaping and spinning to elaborate reels and jigs such as the "Sailor's Hornpipe" or the "Irish Washerwoman."

But in the boiler room, another sort of dance took place. There, anyone who was no one swayed, shovel in hand, to the dark, demanding rhythms of furnace and boiler. Though merriment was produced en masse amongst the well-to-do, and though revelry was abundant for those who sought to cross the ocean and make a new life on a distant shore, it was the incessant dance of the soot-covered boiler men who made possible both the voyage and the celebration.

FATHER BROWNE'S LEGACY

THE GREATEST PICTORIAL RECORD OF THE *TITANIC*

It was the trip of a lifetime for thirty-one-year-old Francis Mary Hegarty Browne, a teacher who had entered the Jesuit seminary in 1897. The future Father Browne had been given an extravagant gift by his Uncle Robert Browne, the Bishop of Cloyne. He was to make a two-day voyage on the *Titanic*, traveling in first-class quarters, from Southampton to Cherbourg, France, and onward to Queenstown (now Cobh), Ireland. Thrilled with the idea, young Francis made sure to pack his early Kodak camera, also a gift from his uncle. The bishop had an eye for talent and a belief in developing one's natural gifts; he thought his nephew such a promising photographer that he installed a darkroom in his house for his nephew's use. The insight proved to have merit. The gift of both trip and camera would serve to leave an indelible passage in the pages of history. The legacy of that brief trip was the world's greatest pictorial record of the great ship, her crew, and passengers.

POLAR, THE *TITANIC* BEAR

The story of six-year-old Douglas Spedden and his toy Steiff bear has captured the imagination of readers young and old. Douglas's mother, Daisy, wrote "My Story" a year after the sinking, as a homemade Christmas storybook for her son. The story emerged in 1986 when one of only two copies of the story she had typed was donated to the *Titanic* Historical Society. The story tells the adventure of the little white bear that toured Europe, was lost at sea, then rescued and reunited with his beloved master. Tragically, the boy survived the *Titanic* only to be killed three years later by one of the early automobiles, when he ran from behind some thick shrubbery into a street. His became the first auto accident death in Maine. This reproduction of the Steiff bear sits next to Father Browne's picture of Douglas in the gallery. The vintage Kodak camera is the same model Father Browne used. The letter from Father Browne to his niece Phillipa is one of only three existing letters written on *Titanic* stationery. *(Camera: Fr. Browne S.J. Collection/Davison & Associates; Letter: Stan Lehrer Collection)*

Father Browne not only captured the final images of the doomed liner departing Queenstown, he recorded as well the gleeful, carefree smiles of many who were soon destined for eternal rest beneath the unforgiving North Atlantic.

Far more than a simple shutterbug, Father Browne came to be known as a master photographer, composing about forty-two thousand images during his lifetime. He was so well-regarded that the head of Kodak, Great Britain, gave him free film for life.

Upon boarding the *Titanic*, the humble man of God was in awe of his surroundings and the immensity of the ship. He reveled in the idea of a luxury cabin complete with bedroom, sitting room, and bathroom with private entrance, but he also immersed himself in the day-to-day life of the crew. Quick to make friends and accepted in areas of the *Titanic* not regularly frequented by his fellow first-class travelers, Father Browne frequently captured in his photos the simplicity of the time and the innermost qualities of his subjects.

Particularly powerful is a photo of Robert Douglas Spedden. The son of wealthy New Yorkers Frederic and Daisy Spedden, six-year-old Douglas happily spins his top on the deck of the *Titanic* as

A master of both technique and sensitive timing, Father Francis Mary Hegarty Browne shot forty-two thousand photos during his lifetime. Today, he is renowned as one of the great photographers of the first half of the twentieth century.
(Father Browne photography from Father Browne S.J. Collection/Davison & Associates)

Happily spinning his top on the *Titanic* deck while his father watches, little Robert Douglas Spedden's merriment is just one of the magical moments captured by Father Francis Browne. It is the only photograph of a child aboard the *Titanic* and is in stark contrast to the coming fight for survival.

his proud father and several other gentlemen look on. The laughing emotion in this cheerful scene is in sharp contrast to what the family undoubtedly felt in the late hours of April 14. Shortly after the collision with the iceberg, the Speddens awakened Helen Wilson, Daisy Spedden's maid, and Elizabeth Burns, Douglas's nanny, whom he called "Muddie Boons." Not wanting to alarm the child, they woke him from sleep, dressed him, and explained they were all were going on deck to look at the stars. Frederic Spedden, unlike many on the *Titanic*, realized that gaining a seat in one of twenty lifeboats was a matter of life and death.

The Speddens, along with both Helen and Elizabeth, survived their nightmare at sea. In 1913, Daisy wrote "My Story," a tale of the family's adventure as told from the viewpoint of Douglas's toy Steiff polar bear. Sadly, little Douglas was killed three years later by an automobile during his summer vacation in Maine.

Father Browne would record innumerable such moments on his voyage. He shot the only known surviving photo of Captain Edward Smith, the bearded master of the ship, peering down from the starboard bridge wing of the *Titanic*. He took the last photo of American short-story writer Jacques Futrelle, who remained aboard the *Titanic* after assuring that his wife was safely aboard a lifeboat. He caught gymnasium steward Thomas McCawley in his white flannels, awaiting those who would seek his assistance and advice in their physical exertions.

Thomas was a native of Aberdeen, Scotland, and had previously worked aboard the *Olympic*. As the *Titanic* began to sink, he is said to have remained in the gym with frightened passengers, speaking calmly about inconsequential matters, doing his utmost to relieve the anxiety of his charges. At one point, it is reported that he refused to don a life belt. When asked why, he explained that he felt it would slow him down, and he felt he had a better chance of survival without it. Perhaps he really believed that, or perhaps he was making one final brave attempt to inspire hope and confidence among the passengers gathered with him in his gym. He did not survive.

These scenes depict but a few of the incredible images taken

Royal Mail Ship

The luxury liner *Titanic* was also a British Royal Mail Ship, designated by the RMS in the official name, the RMS *Titanic*. On her maiden voyage, she carried over thirty-five hundred sacks of mail, which sank with the ship. One can only speculate about consequences of the lost correspondence.

by Father Browne. Through his eye, the hopes and dreams so prevalent on the *Titanic* are projected far into the future. Perhaps more than anything else, his photography personalized a tragedy so enormous that it could otherwise defy comprehension.

In an ironic twist, Father Browne's immortalization of the last days of the *Titanic* could very well have been lost to the whims of fate. When he died on July 7, 1960, his trunk-full of negatives was deposited in the archives of the Irish Jesuits in Dublin. For twenty-five years, they lay untouched, eventually covered by stacks of files and documents. In 1985, Father Eddie O'Donnell opened the trunk and discovered the treasure trove. It was a cache that was priceless both in economic and historical terms.

Other artifacts were also a part of Father Browne's collection. Most notable is a letter he wrote while in transit to Queenstown to his niece Phillipa. It is one of only three existing letters penned on *Titanic* stationery.

"The ship is lovely, and I wish I were going the whole way," he wrote.

Luckily for him — and for the world — he didn't.

UPPER CRUST ENTITLEMENT... *or loving mother?*

Not only did she have an exceptionally long name, Charlotte Wardle Drake Martinez-Cardeza also had an exceptionally large fortune. The child of a Philadelphia fabric manufacturer, she traveled the world on her yacht *Eleanor*, often accompanied by her adult son Thomas. Her marriage to a gentleman of Spanish nobility had ended less than amicably, and in 1912 she and Thomas were returning to America after a safari in Africa. Of course, she booked the most expensive suite on the *Titanic*.

Charlotte and Thomas did not travel light; with them were servants and fourteen steamer trunks of clothing carrying seventy dresses, ninety-one pairs of gloves, and jewelry valued at over $175,000. On the night *Titanic* sank, Charlotte, who had likely never been denied anything in her life, managed to convince crewmen that her son was ill and could not be left on the ship. Unlike many star-crossed male passengers who opted for a dedication to "women and children first," Thomas would gain a lifeboat seat and be rescued with his mother.

This authentic recreation of a third-class cabin shows accommodations that seemed luxurious to many third-class passengers. As visitors view the room, they hear the words of Frankie Goldsmith, age nine, who described the great ship. All the recorded tracks in the museum are the exact words of passengers written before or after the ship sank.

THIRD-CLASS CORRIDOR

LUXURIOUS COMPARED TO OTHER SHIPS

Although they might seem primitive from our modern perspective, third-class accommodations on the *Titanic* surpassed by leaps and bounds the standards of the day. The White Star Line held a reputation for impeccable service, and even the most inexpensive rooms displayed conveniences previously reserved for the upper class. The company was quick to point out this fact in its promotional brochures.

"Third Class quarters are particularly comfortable, up-to-date, spacious and well-arranged. Special attention is paid to the comfort of all passengers in this class. Passengers have commodious and cleanly dining rooms fitted with tables and revolving chairs, a smoking room, and a large number of two- and four-berth staterooms."

Compared to living conditions found on ocean-bound vessels before the *Titanic* and *Olympic*, these words were very true. The small, third-class cabins had berths on both sides of the room; in a four-berth room they were bunk style. The bunks were separated by a wash basin and a container of water. The water was changed daily by the cabin steward, a service which would have been laughable in third class just a few years prior. The rooms also came with heat, electric lights, spring mattresses, blankets, sheets, and pillows. True, there were only two bathtubs for 709 third-class passengers — one for men and one for women — but this was not an oddity in 1912. Daily bathing was not common. Many still viewed the practice as harmful to one's health, and a weekly bath was considered more than sufficient.

TWO PASSENGERS' TALES

Left: Reverend John Harper, front row, second from left, was a Scotsman and widower, raising his six-year-old daughter, Nan. He was a popular preacher for revivals in both Great Britain and America and was on his way to Chicago to preach. This letter shows his ill-fated request to take the *Titanic* rather than the *Lusitania*. Only Nan and her aunt survived. *(Craig Sopin Collection)*

Right: Marshall Drew had just turned eight and was traveling with his aunt and uncle, who were raising him after his mother died when he was only two. They were returning to New York. He shows where he and his aunt, who also survived, were aboard the *Titanic*. He died in 1986. *(Titanic Historical Society/Ed and Karen Kamuda Collection.)*

Chamber pots were located under each berth. Private toilets would have been rare even in first class; toilets as we know them had yet to come into vogue. These chamber pots were emptied daily by cabin stewards, a thankless task. To have a uniformed member of the crew hauling out "slops" must have seemed an unimaginable luxury to the immigrants in third class, many of whom had sold their every possession in order to forge a dream in America.

After all, this was an era when more than a few had grown up on tales of crude ocean travel, the rough conditions and rougher crew, the threat of scurvy, the hard-tack meals, and moldy biscuits.

Even in third class, the pride of the White Star Line was a floating palace.

For dining, third class offered something far better than the splintered benches and short-leg tables of *Titanic's* contemporaries. The third-class dining saloon was simple, but only in comparison to first class. The large room, with enamel-white walls, was actually two rooms separated by a watertight bulkhead. Plates and mugs were of china, perhaps not the most expensive, but still far better than that on which most passengers would have dined in their own homes. Chefs on other ships would have been envious, as even their first-class kitchens paled in comparison to the galleys and pantries that served *Titanic's* least prestigious occupants.

Navigating third class, with berths spread over four separate decks, was not an easy feat. This Minoan maze of corridors, passageways, and stairs did not bode well when disaster struck, for a large percentage of third-class passengers, who represented forty-four different countries, could neither speak, read, nor understand English. Communication without a common language was difficult in the best of times. As *Titanic* took on water and panic set in, the translation of routes, directions, and information became virtually impossible.

While tales of heroism and cowardice of those in third class are not nearly as well known as those of the rich and famous in first class, they are no less inspiring and anguished.

Little Elizabeth Gladys "Millvina" Dean was just nine weeks old when she boarded *Titanic* with her parents, Bertram and Hetty, and two-year-old brother Bertram Dean, Jr. Her father was relocating the family to Wichita, Kansas, where he intended to open a cigar store. Though the Deans had originally booked passage on another ship, an English coal strike led to the cancellation of that voyage and their reassignment to the *Titanic*.

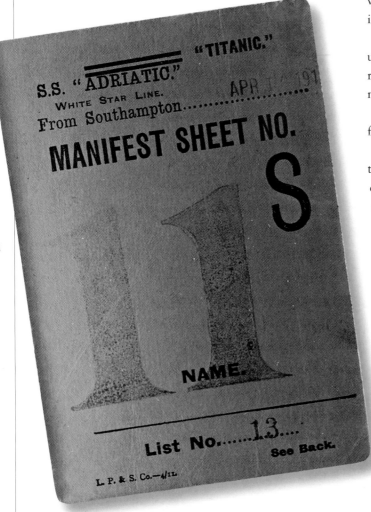

INSPECTION CARD

All passengers carried inspection cards, which served as both boarding pass and medical clearance. A similar one would have been carried by Einar Karlsson, a twenty-one-year-old third-class passenger traveling from Sweden to New York. Einar loved the sea and grew up around fishing boats and small ships. After his discharge from the Swedish army, he decided to visit America. He traveled to England, intending to board the *Adriatic*. But a coal strike in England resulted in his transfer to the *Titanic*. The young man shared a four-berth cabin forward in the bow of F deck. Einar walked about the decks to acquaint himself with the layout, and he later told people that knowledge saved his life. *(Titanic Historical Society/Ed and Karen Kamuda Collection)*

The death of children was particularly tragic. Ninety-four children in third class were under fifteen years of age; sixty-three perished. Likewise, the survival of children, especially, was celebrated with passion. The two "Titanic Tots," as the world came to know them, were a real mystery. A handwritten note on the back of the photo shown above reads, "...picked up almost naked — an open boat by the *Carpathia* crewmen. ... Both children are wearing borrowed clothes." Ages three and two, they were shocked into silence and did not understand English. Self-appointed custodian, wealthy New Yorker Margaret Hays, twenty-four, spoke French fluently, which later helped her communicate with her young wards. Slowly, the puzzle was solved. The tots' father, Frenchman Michel Navratil, soon-to-be-divorced, had taken his sons secretly and was traveling under an assumed name. Their mother, Marcelle, was eventually located and reunited with her sons, Michel and Edmond. *(Stan Lehrer Collection)* Twenty-four rollers throughout the museum test the knowledge of children today about the *Titanic*.

The Overlooked Class

Tales abound of the elite who traveled in *Titanic*'s first-class accommodations, and because so many met their deaths, we often hear the legends of ill-fated third-class passengers.

WHAT WAS LIFE LIKE IN SECOND CLASS?

Second-class passengers tended to be neither terribly wealthy nor terribly poor. They were the middle class, professionals, teachers, some of the more well-to-do immigrants, and even a smattering of those who simply didn't care for the elaborate social posturing of first class. Second class was, in fact, extremely ornate, with impressive cabins, woodcarvings, and unique patterns in the ceiling fixtures. The dining room was capable of seating four hundred and was oak-paneled in the early English style. More than seventy feet long, it covered nearly the full width of the ship and was furnished with long tables and revolving, carved chairs, which were bolted to the floor. The revolving chairs made it easy to socialize with people at other tables. The second-class smoking room was decorated in Louis XIV style with oak paneling and dado in relief. Heavy oak chairs were upholstered in dark green Moroccan leather. Finally, a highly ornamental library with neo-Gothic details, Roman motifs, and complex color schemes was the main social room of second class. It provided a warm and inviting atmosphere for socializing, writing letters, or general relaxation. Paneled in sycamore with carved mahogany dado, this room and numerous other amenities made second-class passengers feel they were reclining in the lap of luxury herself.

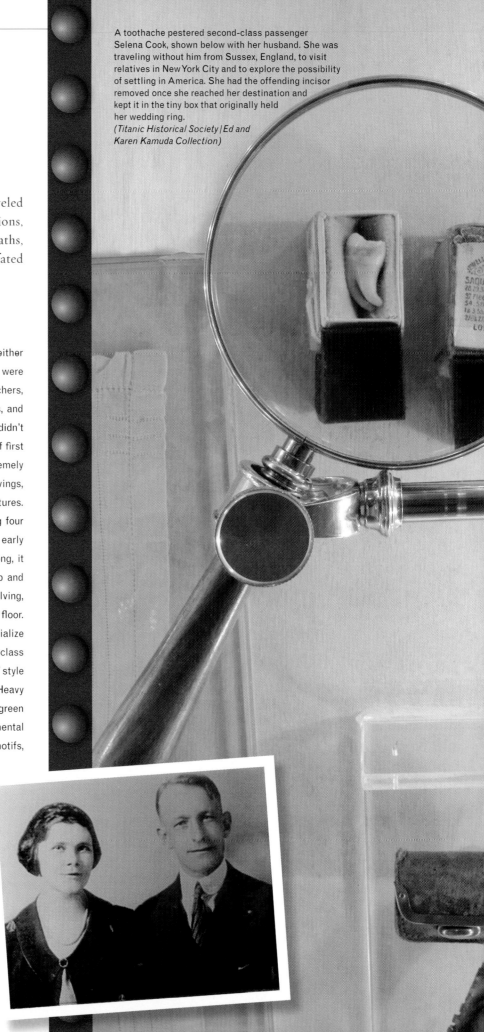

A toothache pestered second-class passenger Selena Cook, shown below with her husband. She was traveling without him from Sussex, England, to visit relatives in New York City and to explore the possibility of settling in America. She had the offending incisor removed once she reached her destination and kept it in the tiny box that originally held her wedding ring.
(Titanic Historical Society/Ed and Karen Kamuda Collection)

SMALL TREASURES

This button is from a *Titanic* mess steward's uniform. Cecil Fitzpatrick survived by clinging to an overturned lifeboat; he later gave it to survivor Lillian Bentham Black in gratitude. Nearing death from hypothermia, Fitzpatrick blew his scout whistle and attracted Lifeboat 12. Lillian placed her fur coat around the freezing man. The comb and purse at left and the milk-glass souvenir plate above belonged to Selena Cook. The museum also has her handkerchief, a piece of stationery, and one of only three envelopes known to exist that were postmarked on the *Titanic*. (*Titanic Historical Society/Ed and Karen Kamuda Collection*)

Bertram Dean Sr. felt the *Titanic* ram the iceberg and hurried the family to the upper decks. Like many brave men, he remained aboard ship to make room for women and children in the lifeboats. He died in the disaster, but Millvina, her brother Bertram, and Hetty would all survive their ordeal. As for little Millvina, she was heralded in the press as "the Miracle Baby," and passengers from all classes on the rescue ship *Carpathia* lined up simply to hold her.

Today (2006), she is one of only two living survivors of the *Titanic*. In her mid-nineties, she never married and continues to reside in Southampton, from which her family embarked in April of 1912.

A similar tale is that of the ill-fated Goldsmith family. Emily and Frank Goldsmith were the last of their siblings to immigrate from England to America. Even though their family across the ocean wrote often of the opportunities to be had in the West, the couple nonetheless preferred to remain in their home country. But their attachment to England was loosened in Christmas, 1911, when their youngest child died of diphtheria. Devastated, the Goldsmiths sought a new life, embarking with their nine-year-old son, Frankie, on an exodus to Detroit, Michigan.

Frankie loved the *Titanic*, and with other boys his age, explored as much of the massive ship as was allowed. On the night of the collision, he awoke to find his mother dressing him. In later years, Frankie recalled that, even amidst the chaos, he thought the opportunity to ride in a lifeboat would be a grand adventure.

The Goldsmith family headed toward the boat deck, negotiating crowded passages with Frankie's help, and even climbing a steel ladder. Their hopes for a complete escape were smashed when, at a gateway, Frank was held back by crewmen. Staring death in the eye, he refused to blink; he would not further frighten his child. Frank handled himself with the sort of calm demeanor usually associated with the battle-hardened. He kissed his wife, put his arm around his son, and said, "So long, Frankie, I'll see you later."

Son and mother would live to see land, but Frank, as with so many others, went down with the *Titanic*.

Because 528 of the 709 third-class passengers perished, artifacts from that class are incredibly rare. The museum contains a few items from the Goldsmiths and other families.

One of the most poignant of these items was retrieved by the rescue ship *Mackay-Bennett,* which also performed the grisly work of recovering 306 bodies. Upon opening the small trunk they retrieved from the water, the *Mackay-Bennett* crew found nothing but a small purse, a bracelet, and a blue blouse, which had been altered many times. The woman to whom these items

R.M.S. TITANIC

THE MACKAY-BENNETT RECOVERED
306 BODIES. THIS HALF LIFE JACKET
WAS CUT FROM AN UNIDENTIFIED BODY
OF WHICH 116 WERE BURIED AT SEA.

RECOVERED FROM THE OCEAN

The salvage ship *Mackay-Bennett* recovered 306 bodies and many other items, including this trunk, from the floating debris field of the *Titanic*. The crew didn't find much inside: a small purse, a bracelet, and this blue blouse. The blouse showed much wear and had been altered many times, suggesting that the owner was a frugal third-class immigrant. It remains a mystery as to whether the woman who once prized these few possessions lived or died. Her meager belongings are now worth more than thirty-two thousand dollars. *(Cedar Bay Entertainment Collection)*

belonged was never identified, but judging by her few possessions and the much-altered blouse, it is likely she was a third-class passenger who had scraped together just enough money to begin a life in America. It is ironic that, now, these three simple articles are valued at more than thirty-two thousand dollars.

Last but far from least, no account of third class would be complete without the woeful narrative of the Sage family. John Sage and his oldest son, George, had traveled to Canada in 1910 and found work on a farm. Industrious men, over the next two years they managed to save enough money to buy a citrus grove in the vicinity of Jacksonville, Florida. Thus it was that, in April of 1912, John and his wife, Annie, boarded the *Titanic* with children George, Stella, Douglas, Frederick, Anthony, Elizabeth, Constance, Dorothy, and Thomas. The children ranged in age from five to twenty, and the close-knit clan was cheerfully ensconced in third class when they felt the *Titanic* shudder.

The entire family hurriedly made their way to the boat deck, and Stella, the oldest, secured a seat in a lifeboat. She waited and waited for the rest of the family to join her, but minutes passed with no sign. Whether she left the lifeboat to search for her kin or whether she felt she could not bear a life without her loved ones will never be known. What is known is that Stella stepped back to the deck, relinquishing her lifeboat spot to another, and sealed her fate.

Not a single member of the Sage family survived.

This 1910 woman's watch is similar to the one third-class immigrant women might have worn. Women from all over the Old World were traveling to America to join husbands or other relatives to begin new lives in what was described as a land of opportunity. *(Cedar Bay Entertainment Collection)*

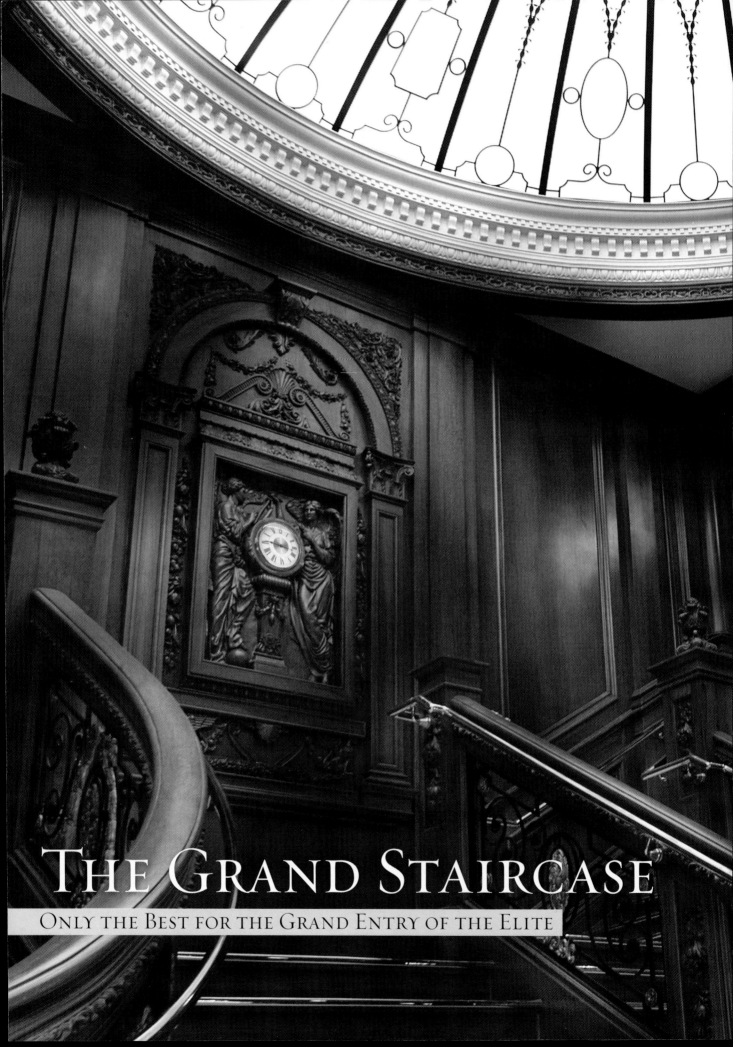

THE GRAND STAIRCASE
Only the Best for the Grand Entry of the Elite

MAGNIFICENT FULL-SCALE REPLICA

The Grand Staircase, replicated accurately and full-scale in the museum, was the perfect mesh of art, form, and function. The stairs at the museum were built in California and reassembled at Branson. Woodworkers and iron workers recreated with accurate detail the exquisite oak wood carvings and wrought-iron balustrades. There were actually two Grand Staircases onboard the *Titanic*, one forward and one aft. The one forward contained the famous *Honour and Glory Crowning Time* clock carving. Submersible cameras that explored the *Titanic*'s watery grave in 1987 found both the cherub light, lying eerily dark, as well as the clock carving.

RICH WOODWORK

The allegory *Honour and Glory Crowning Time* was intricately carved into huge oak panels that graced the uppermost landings of both the *Titanic* and the *Olympic*. The one onboard the *Olympic* is displayed in a museum at Southampton, England. Ironically, the clock now seems to symbolize the story of the great ship that ran out of time.

Pineapples, native to South America, became a symbol of hospitality in Europe and colonial America, after they were brought back from the Caribbean by Christopher Columbus. The elaborately carved pineapple newel posts welcomed first-class passengers at the base and landings of the Grand Staircase.

The most imposing structure in first class, without any doubt, was the Grand Staircase. Constructed of solid oak, it reached sixty feet high and served five decks, from Deck A with the first-class lounge and reading and writing room, through Decks B and C, with various other first-class accommodations, to Deck D, with the first-class reception room and dining salon, to Deck E with the first-class staterooms. Natural sunlight shone down upon the painstakingly carved balustrades via a massive dome of wrought iron and glass. At night, as the ambience of first class never slept, the skylight was electrically illuminated. The most well-known details of the Grand Staircase, both popularized in the movie by James Cameron and still visible in the remains of the *Titanic* twelve thousand feet below the surface of the Atlantic, are a cherub light at the foot of the stairs and a clock at the uppermost landing. The stairs themselves appear to be fashioned of the finest marble. In fact, since the *Titanic*'s designers spared no expense to outfit the ship with the very best products of the time, they covered the steps with the revolutionary new product known as linoleum, used in the most elite décor in 1912.

ELABORATE AND ORNATE

Details on the *Titanic* were highly decorative and extravagant, such as the gilted gold medallions on the balustrade surrounding the Grand Staircase. In an earlier time, most staircases had lamp standards at the bottom for practical reasons. The bronze cherub holding the lamp on the Grand Staircase would have been for ornamental purposes, as the ship was well-lit by crystal chandeliers and the skylight, which was electrified to simulate daylight even at night. A cherub has been recovered from the wreck of the *Titanic*, but it is one of a pair of smaller cherubs that were mounted at the side of the staircase. Uniformed reenactors such as first-class maid Jaynee, at right, answer museum guests' questions.

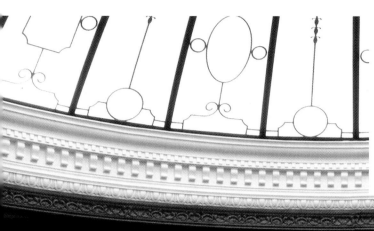

A MIX OF STYLES

The Grand Staircase contains woodwork in the William-and-Mary style, named after the monarchs who reigned jointly in the late 1600s. The style is characterized by tall and slender elements, with many scroll, spiral, and columnar shapes. William-and-Mary style is itself an interpretation of the baroque style that had swept Europe a century before. The ormolu garlands on the wrought-iron balustrades were inspired by the French court of Louis XIV. Gilded crystal chandeliers glittered throughout first-class rooms. Today, visitors walking down the staircase see exactly what first-class passengers would have seen, except for the modern brass safety railings.

Private baths were a luxury even for the wealthy who traveled in *Titanic's* first-class staterooms. The White Star Line used this image to promote the opulence of their newest ships, the *Olympic* and the *Titanic*.

FIRST-CLASS STATEROOM

JOHN JACOB ASTOR IV OCCUPIED A SUITE FIT FOR A KING

Without question, the wealthiest man on the *Titanic* was Colonel John Jacob Astor IV. Heir to an estate of nearly one hundred million dollars, he was the personification of American royalty. Though not as famous as his great-grandfather, who built the family fortune via fur trading and real estate, John had established himself in a number of diverse fields. In 1894, he wrote an early science fiction novel, *A Journey in Other Worlds*, which imagined life in the year 2000 on the planets Saturn and Jupiter. He invented a bicycle brake, helped develop a turbine engine, and built the legendary Astoria Hotel in Manhattan. In later years, the Astoria would be joined with the Waldorf Hotel next door, built by John's cousin, William Waldorf Astor, to become the Waldorf-Astoria complex.

No stranger to risk, John had volunteered to fight in Cuba during the Spanish-American War in 1898 and financed an entire battalion from his own pocket. He was appointed a lieutenant-colonel of his battalion, and thereafter was known as Colonel Astor. But, in 1912, he was facing another sort of opponent. He had divorced his first wife and then married an eighteen-year-old woman, Madeleine Force, in 1911. John and his young bride had become the target of the wagging tongues of the northeast coast's social elite. The union of the forty-seven-year-old

REPLICA OF ASTOR'S SUITE

The museum's first-class stateroom is an exact replica of one of four suites John Jacob Astor reserved. It was not unusual for first-class passengers to book several adjoining rooms to provide plenty of space for servants, children, or entertaining. A button to summon a steward for room service would be discreetly hidden on a column.

and his teen bride caused such a scandal amongst the upper crust that the couple traveled to Egypt on an extended honeymoon, hoping to return when the scandal had worn out its novelty. However, when Madeleine discovered she was pregnant with her first child, the Astors immediately decided to return to New York.

If you are an Astor, then you travel in accommodations befitting an Astor. In this case, it seems almost a given that the honeymooners chose to sail on the most opulent liner of the day. They were accustomed to the best, and nothing surpassed the luxurious first-class staterooms of the "unsinkable" *Titanic*.

These suites were regarded as being "fit for a king." As reported by *The Shipbuilder* magazine shortly before the *Titanic* embarked on her maiden voyage, first-class staterooms included "two bedsteads, an addressing table, wash basin, sofa, easy chair and free-standing wardrobe." Some suites featured separate wardrobe rooms, a writing table, and additional furniture. The interior design found in first-class rooms could vary; styles such as Empire, Italian Renaissance, Queen Anne, Adams, Louis XVI, Dutch, and Old Dutch Empire were all represented. Elegant touches and a dedication to the finest examples of craftsmanship could be found in first class. Columns featured ornate carvings, and the floors were covered with a high-grade carpeting.

The Astors surely imagined that the journey back to America would offer the rejuvenation of fresh salt air and the pampering to which they were accustomed. Boarding the *Titanic* in Cherbourg, John and Madeleine were accompanied by their manservant, maid, and Kitty, the colonel's pet Airedale. Also traveling with them was Margaret "Molly" Brown. Margaret had been one of the few socialites who did not shun the Astors after their marriage. Having come from humble beginnings in Hannibal, Missouri, Molly regarded the attitudes of high society with more than a grain of salt. She had joined the couple in their travels from Egypt to France.

On the night of April 14, when the *Titanic* rammed into the iceberg, John did not at first believe the situation to be serious. He simply returned to his lavish quarters in first class, assuming that all was well. This mistaken belief would not

The addressing table was a standard feature of a first-class stateroom. Complete with an ornate electric lamp and fine writing tools, the writing desk reminded passengers they were traveling on a vessel of unsurpassed grace and style.

have been far-fetched, considering the size of the *Titanic* and her reputation for being unsinkable.

Soon, though, the truth made itself evident; the *Titanic* was sinking. John first took the frightened Madeleine to the ship's gymnasium and cut open a life belt so that she might see the buoyant materials that would keep her afloat. From there, the Astors headed to the boat deck, where John helped his young bride into a lifeboat. He asked an officer in charge if he might join her, noting her "delicate condition," but the officer insisted that no man could board until all the women and children were safe and away.

John, displaying a great sense of honor, wholly accepted this mandate. He simply asked for the number of the lifeboat, tossed his gloves to Madeleine, and lit a cigarette. While Madeleine and her maid, Rosalie Bidois, survived the sinking, Colonel John Astor and his manservant, and presumably Kitty the Airedale, perished. On April 22, John's battered body was recovered by the *Mackay-Bennett*. His pockets contained nearly twenty-five hundred dollars and a gold watch.

Madeleine Astor had a son, John Jacob V, the following August. Though she was still wealthy, provided with the annual investment income from a five-million-dollar trust fund, neither Madeleine nor her son would ever again travel in such style as was found in first class on the *Titanic*. According to the wishes of John's will, the bulk of his one-hundred-million-dollar estate was left to his eldest son, Vincent, born during his first marriage to Philadelphia socialite Ava Lowle Willing. Vincent was a year older than his father's new bride.

It is said that Vincent carried the recovered watch of his beloved father till the day of his own death in 1959.

First-class passengers could take one of three elevators between decks. Second class had one elevator; third-class passengers took the stairs. The museum elevator exactly duplicates a first-class elevator, down to the buttons. The same attention to detail and fine quality woodwork can be seen even in the elevator. One elevator opened into the first-class reception room of the *Titanic*, just off the Grand Staircase and adjoining the dining salon. While one imagines the grand entries on the staircase, in 1912, the titans on the *Titanic* might have preferred this technological luxury.

The only surviving carpet sample

Frederic Ray Dent, saloon steward on the *Titanic*, happened to be on hand when the carpeting was being laid in the giant ship's first-class staterooms. The date was April 2, 1912, and Frederic could not resist taking a swatch of the lush green floor covering home. "I wanted my wife to see the lovely carpets they are putting on the grand ship," he later explained.

Frederic survived, and understandably, the piece of carpet he had squirreled away was the furthest thing from his mind. Fifty years later, while preparing to move to new quarters, he picked up the piano stool he had long ago made for his wife. It was then that it hit him — the padding for that stool was that forgotten square of carpet. He took off the stool cover, and the carpet was as good as new.

This is the only surviving sample of carpet from the *Titanic*.

FIRST-CLASS DINING SALON

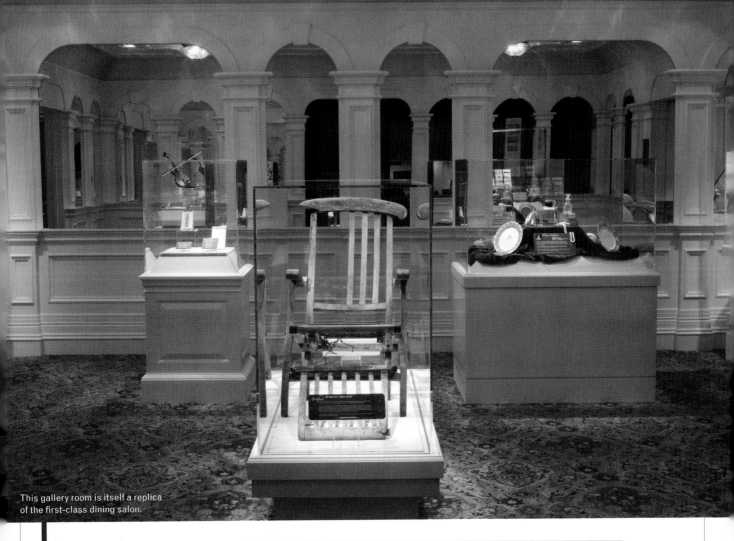

This gallery room is itself a replica of the first-class dining salon.

FORMAL DINNERS, HAUTE COUTURE, AND DESIGNER CHINA

Class distinctions were an accepted fact of life in the Edwardian era, but nowhere was the chasm between the "haves" and "have-nots" more conspicuous than in the first-class dining salon of the *Titanic*. Although all meals on the great liner were served at the same hour (breakfast from 8:30 to 10:30 AM; lunch from 1 to 2:30 PM; and dinner from 6 to 7:30 PM), the locations in which passengers enjoyed their repast were worlds apart.

The first-class dining salon was unparalleled both in size and luxury, surpassing many of the finest restaurants in Europe. This was where first-class passengers came to see and be seen, to mingle, to discuss their acquisitions, and to partake of the very latest in scandalous gossip. This was where riches were on full display, a place where diamonds glittered on every hand and small talk took on the countenance of a contact sport. It was *the* place to impress and be impressed.

This priceless 1912 glacé silk gown with hand-made lace is a rare surviving original designed by world-renowned couturière Lucy, Lady Duff Gordon. Handmade floral sprays were a distinctive signature feature that signaled the creation as an expensive "Lucile" gown. The museum also has a black silk-draped tea gown with a Lucile Ltd. label on loan. *(Lewis Orchard, Lucile Ltd. Collection)*

Stretching the full ninety-two-foot width of the ship, the dining salon encompassed a total of 10,488 square feet and was capable of accommodating 550 passengers per sitting. In appearance, the effect was one of entering the formal dining room of a grand English estate. Numerous recessed bays were built into the walls, allowing passengers to enjoy their gourmet entrees with a modicum of privacy, and lights were designed to give the impression of a bright and sunny day. To further enhance the merry aesthetics, intricately molded ceilings and walls painted in soft white hues served as a counterpoint to classic solid-oak furniture. At the front of the room, of course, was the Captain's Table. With seating for six, an invitation to dine with Captain Edward Smith was a sought-after prize.

More than sixty chefs and chef's assistants worked to prepare exquisite feasts, their specialties ranging from soups and sauces to desserts, pastries, wild game, and a cornucopia of gourmet delights. A kosher chef was onboard for those Jewish passengers who required kosher food.

The reception room where all passengers congregated before the dinner hour joined the dining salon and was fifty-four-feet long and also covered the full width of the ship. Nearly as luxurious as the dining salon and including a grand piano, it was here where the blue bloods of society first gathered for conversation, social niceties, and no small amount of posturing.

Many of the refined ladies in first-class arrived for dinner dressed in one of the latest styles from Lucile Limited. With its headquarters in London and branches in Paris and New York, the revered line of gowns produced by "Lucile" was the very height of fashion. A well-dressed woman in first-class might float into the reception room bedecked in a cloud of pink glacé silk, handmade lace, and floral sprays, her gown a thing of envy to those wearing one procured from a lesser designer. If she was hosting a private dinner within her cabin, perhaps for family members or trusted friends, she might choose a black, silk-draped tea gown with silk tassels. Though formal, this gown was the talk of the fashion world. Created from a single piece of fabric and patterned so as not to require a restrictive corset, it would not have been worn in the formal dining room, but rather, in a lady's own cabin at a private supper or tea with intimate friends.

GLASS CRUET

White Star First Class glass cruet. *Titanic* provides an exquisite microcosm of the Edwardian world, illuminating its strict class distinctions, its obsession with etiquette and fashion and, inevitably, its love of fine food.
• *Cedar Bay Entertainment Collection* •

This demitasse cup and saucer are a rare example of the first-class dinner service. Spode of England, one of the world's finest porcelain makers, created the service exclusively for *Titanic*. The butter pat server and knife are from the White Star Line, and the knife is marked for kosher service. This menu cover was actually misprinted with the three-masted White Star Line training ship *Mersey* shown. (*Cup, butter tray, butter knife, and cruet: Cedar Bay Entertainment Collection; saucer: Titanic Concepts Inc. Collection; menu: Stan Lehrer Collection.*)

The Last Supper

Private dinner parties were popular, too. Eleanor Elkins Widener and her husband, George, one of America's foremost financiers and their son, Harry, hosted the only major affair of that kind on the night of the sinking, for some of the wealthiest guests and in honor of Captain Smith. He excused himself about 9 PM to go to the bridge, where everything was about to go wrong.

After the collision, Eleanor emphatically demanded to remain onboard with her husband and son, but they just as emphatically placed her aboard Lifeboat Number 4. She never saw them again.

Deck Chairs

This is one of the only deck chairs in the world that matches those seen in Father Browne's *Titanic* photos, which show literally hundreds of these chairs lining the first-class decks, some with cane seats, some with slat. This Nantucket-style chair, made of teak, is now valued at $135,000. It was pulled from the sea by a crewman on one of the salvage ships. *(Titanic Concepts Inc. Collection)*

Waters Cannot Quench Love

German emigrant Isador Straus made a fortune as a successful retail merchandiser in the United States. He founded Macy's and served in Congress. He and his wife, Ida, were returning after a holiday on the Riviera. When ordered into a lifeboat, Ida refused. Handing her fur coat to her personal maid, Ellen Bird, she stepped aside, holding her husband's hand tightly. They were last seen clasped in an embrace.

Solomon Small and H.A. Russotto wrote this commemorative song with Yiddish lyrics for Ida and Isador. The cover includes a sketch of their faces. They are also memorialized by a monument in New York at Broadway and 106th Street that has this inscription, "Many waters cannot quench love, neither can the floods drown it." *(Stan Lehrer Collection)*

The gowns produced by Lucile Limited were all the more popular on the *Titanic* because the namesake of the company was onboard herself. Lucy, Lady Duff Gordon, founder of the renowned firm "Lucile," was the premier fashion maven of the age.

Lucy was, quite simply, both the Martha Stewart and Vera Wang of her day. She was the first to grasp the concept of branding a product and to invent the runway-style fashion show as well as the slit skirt. Her second marriage, to Sir Cosmo Duff Gordon, had brought her happiness, wealth, and fame. Sir Cosmo, the Fifth Baronet of Halkin, was known for his love of sports and was an extremely popular figure in both England and his native Scotland. Not only had he participated as a champion fencer in both the 1906 and 1908 Olympics, he had also founded the London Fencing Club. The couple was traveling to Lucy's New York branch to conduct business, accompanied by Lucy's secretary, Laura Francatelli.

But gowns, fashion, and social status lost their importance as the *Titanic* began taking on water. The Duff Gordons made their way to the boat deck. They and their maid secured seats on a lifeboat and were lowered into the water. All would survive the tragedy but not without numerous questions as to the actions of Sir Cosmo.

Lucy and Sir Cosmo were the only *Titanic* passengers who were called to testify at the British Board of Trade inquiries into the sinking. The Duff Gordons were forced to defend themselves against accusations that they had commandeered a lifeboat by bribery. The primary charge was that Sir Cosmo promised five pounds sterling to every lifeboat passenger to prevent its return to the site of the disaster; it was suggested he feared a rescue attempt might cause the craft to be capsized by the frantic survivors who floundered in the frigid Atlantic.

The Duff Gordons were never formally charged with any wrongdoing, and Lucile Limited continued to be an immensely popular brand. In 1916, Lucy contracted with Sears Roebuck to offer lower-priced versions of her styles via mail order.

Wealth and fame can be fleeting. Lucy lost a massive lawsuit and declared personal bankruptcy in 1922. Sir Cosmo died in 1931.

But the Grand Dame of fashion did manage to have a last word. In 1932, three years before she succumbed to breast cancer and pneumonia, Lucy published an autobiography, *Discretions and Indiscretions*.

Whether all the indiscretions of Lord and Lady Duff Gordon were included can perhaps only be answered by their long-gone fellow lifeboat survivors.

And the Band Played On

The *Titanic*'s bandmaster, thirty-three-year-old Wallace Hartley, was a trained violinist who had led orchestras in a variety of English towns. The native of Colne, Lancashire, England, had been a band member on the Cunard liner *Mauretania* before accepting the position of bandmaster on the *Titanic*.

In 1912, Wallace had recently become engaged to a young woman in Boston Spa, Yorkshire, England. He spent the entire week before the departure of the *Titanic* with his bride-to-be.

Wallace was the epitome of cool, calm, and collected, displaying what can only be described as courage under fire. As the *Titanic* began to sink, he and the rest of the band members came to the deck and played songs to calm the passengers. Most of these tunes were the lively sort, in the new Ragtime style. It had to be a surreal vision; the music from such innovative composers as Scott Joplin rang out to the ears of two thousand people in the throes of justifiable panic.

Wallace and the band played on until the final plunge of the great liner. Those in the lifeboats commented in later years that they would never forget the sound, a mesh of sweet music and screaming voices traveling over the waves.

And then, finally, there was silence.

THE BOYS IN THE BAND

While it is bandmaster Wallace Hartley that is best remembered as a hero of the *Titanic*, the musicians who performed with him displayed equal courage. They were:

W. Theodore Brailey, Pianist, of Notting Hill, England

Roger Bricoux, Cellist, of Lille, France

John Frederick Clarke, Bass Violist, of Liverpool, England

John Law "Jock" Hume, First Violinist, of Dumfries, Scottland

George Krins, Violinist, of Brixton, England

Percy Cornelius Taylor, Cellist and Pianist, of Clapham, England

John Wesley Woodward, Cellist, of Headington, Oxon, England

THE LAST SONG

It has long been reported that the final song played by Wallace Hartley's band was "Nearer, My God, To Thee." The song was new in 1912, so this is a possibility, but historians and researchers believe the story is myth. Rather, most credible researchers believe the band played lively ragtime music and that the final song performed before *Titanic* sank was the popular hit "Songe d' Automne," by Archibald Joyce.

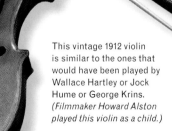

This vintage 1912 violin is similar to the ones that would have been played by Wallace Hartley or Jock Hume or George Krins. *(Filmmaker Howard Alston played this violin as a child.)*

The Luxury of First Class

If you have to ask how much it costs, you can't afford it. This holds true as much today as it did in 1912. If you compare the rates charged for the most exquisite rooms on the *Titanic* to the most luxurious and expensive hotels and resorts of today, the *Titanic* rates are still much higher. Royalty and the wealthy titans of commerce paid those rates.

For instance, in 2006, you could travel to Rania, a new resort in Maldives, and easily drop ten thousand dollars per night — and a three-night stay is required. At The Atlantis on Paradise Island in the Bahamas, for a mere twenty-five thousand dollars per night, you will enjoy your own butler, bar, and ten-room suite. The Imperial Suite at the President Wilson hotel in Geneva, Switzerland, will set you back only twenty-four thousand dollars per night. The Presidential Suite at the legendary Plaza in Manhattan seems a bargain at only fifteen thousand dollars per night. At the Fairmont in San Francisco, the pittance of ten thousand dollars an evening will reserve the penthouse suite.

But this is pocket change.

A first-class parlor suite on the *Titanic*, when adjusted for inflation, surpassed the fifty-thousand-dollar mark. There were only four of these parlor suites on the ship, all containing two bedrooms, a sitting room, and a private bath, which was virtually unheard of in the early days of the twentieth century. Little surprise, Bruce Ismay, the managing director of the White Star Line, booked three of this quartet of ultimate accommodations. Of course, Mr. Ismay may have received an insider's discount.

Regular first-class staterooms were far more affordable. These rooms could be connected, were elegant in their own right, and cost only $1,724 apiece in 1912 currency.

Keep in mind that your average worker of the era, such as the folks who built the *Titanic* in the Harland and Wolff shipyard, earned at most forty dollars per month (roughly $425 in 2006 figures).

When the time came to take a stroll, those in first class could either walk the Boat or Promenade Decks. The latter, covered for the convenience of passengers, did not run the entire length of the ship. However, it did provide access to various rooms and services to which those at the pinnacle of the social ladder were accustomed. These included the first-class reading and writing room, the first-class lounge, the first-class smoking room, and the Palm Court, which was a cafe.

Several features incorporated into *Titanic*'s design had never before been included on an ocean liner. The swimming pool, squash courts, Turkish baths, and gymnasium were all innovative concepts for a cruise ship. The Turkish baths, reserved strictly for first-class passengers, were available at different times for men and women; the *Titanic* may have been a trendsetter, but co-ed hot tubs were definitely taboo. The same rules applied to the swimming pool; men and women splashing about in a state of partial undress, no matter the size of their assets, was simply not done. The *Titanic* gymnasium contained the latest in exercise equipment, such as rowing machines and stationary bikes, and, again, was available for the ladies and gentlemen at separate hours. Surprisingly for those times, the gymnasium also set aside periods exclusively for children.

And then there was the pursuit of Epicurean delights. Aside from the elaborate first-class dining room and reception area already described, the *Titanic* offered the Veranda Cafe, also known as the Palm Court. While not a restaurant per se, this small area with its bright furniture, climbing plants, and seven-foot-high, bronze–framed windows was a popular relaxation spot which created the illusion of an English summer garden.

The Café Parisian was exactly what the name implied, an authentic reproduction of an

FIRST-CLASS PASSENGERS ENJOYED A READING AND WRITING ROOM, A LOUNGE, AND A SMOKING ROOM.

First-class passengers could enjoy the glass-enclosed promenade and features never before seen on an ocean liner, such as a swimming pool, squash courts, Turkish baths, and a fully outfitted gymnasium. The dainty slippers are from the rare Lucile Ltd. collection. Margaret "Molly" Brown presented the Ushabiti talisman to the Captain of the *Carpathia*. These ancient Egyptian statues were found in tombs and thought to have magical powers. *(Slippers: Lewis Orchard, Lucile Ltd. Collection; Ushabiti: Stan Lehrer Collection)*

outdoor Paris bistro. Both dinners and lunches were served at this cafe, with orders taken and delivered by French waiters.

However, the supreme haven for the connoisseur with a refined palate was the A la Carte Restaurant. In this gastronomic Garden of Eden, those in first class could partake of culinary creations that bordered on the sensual. The walls of French walnut and the colorful floral arrangements upon the tables served to accentuate the appetizers, entrees, and desserts created by internationally renowned restaurateur Luigi Gatti, and the room was perfect for

either small, romantic meals or large, elaborate dinner parties.

Luigi, who had previously headed two separate Ritz restaurants, went so far as to bring along all of his own staff, from chefs to waiters and wine butlers. Many were members of his own family, and sadly, Luigi and all but one of the A la Carte's kitchen staff perished in the disaster that was to come.

We can only assume that both they and the passengers who relished the expertise of the *Titanic*'s superb chefs, enjoyed the most libertine of final repasts.

THE MARCONI ROOM

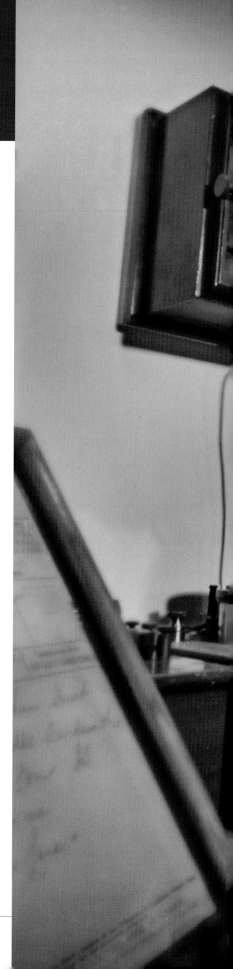

When we think of life-saving innovations, our minds generally conjure up discoveries from the field of medicine. We might recall Edward Jenner's smallpox vaccine, Jonas Salk's advances against polio, or the first successful heart transplant by Dr. Christiaan Barnard. Rarely though would we name those who originated such wonders as the seat belt, thought of by George Cayley in the 1800s; the smoke detector, created by Kenneth House and Randolph Smith in 1969; or long-range wireless communication, invented by Guglielmo Marconi in 1897.

This is an oversight, for if not for Marconi, the 712 survivors of the *Titanic* would have most likely perished.

Marconi, an Italian-Irish electrical engineer and Nobel laureate, developed the first reliable system of wireless telegraphy. In December of 1901, this "Father of Radio" succeeded in receiving a transatlantic, wireless signal in St. John's, Newfoundland. Both a shrewd businessman and a brilliant inventor, Marconi continued to perfect his device and enhance its range, placing wireless stations in key locations and offering his apparatus for installation in ocean-going vessels. By the time 1902 came to a close, he had established twenty-five land stations and placed a Marconi Room in more than seventy ships.

For those in this century, a time when most people under the age of thirty cannot conceive of even an old-style rotary phone, the absence of instant communication seems an impossibility; the meteoric ascent of cell phones, wireless internet, Blackberries, and Palm Pilots has transformed person-to-person contact into a nearly autonomic response. But, barely more than a century ago, the only form of wireless communication available required a complex array of noisy equipment, highly trained operators, and simple messages tapped out in Morse code. Before that, a ship at sea was, quite simply, isolated from the world. In case of a disaster, the only recourse was to pray and hope for safe harbor. Should the craft sink, any knowledge of her fate as well as the fate of her passengers would remain forever a mystery.

No surprise then, as the most technologically up-to-date liner of her day, the *Titanic* possessed the very finest wireless Marconi Room that money could buy. The men who administered the revolutionary machine were not considered part of the *Titanic*'s normal crew. Instead, they were employees of the Marconi Company itself, assigned by rotation to operate the equipment.

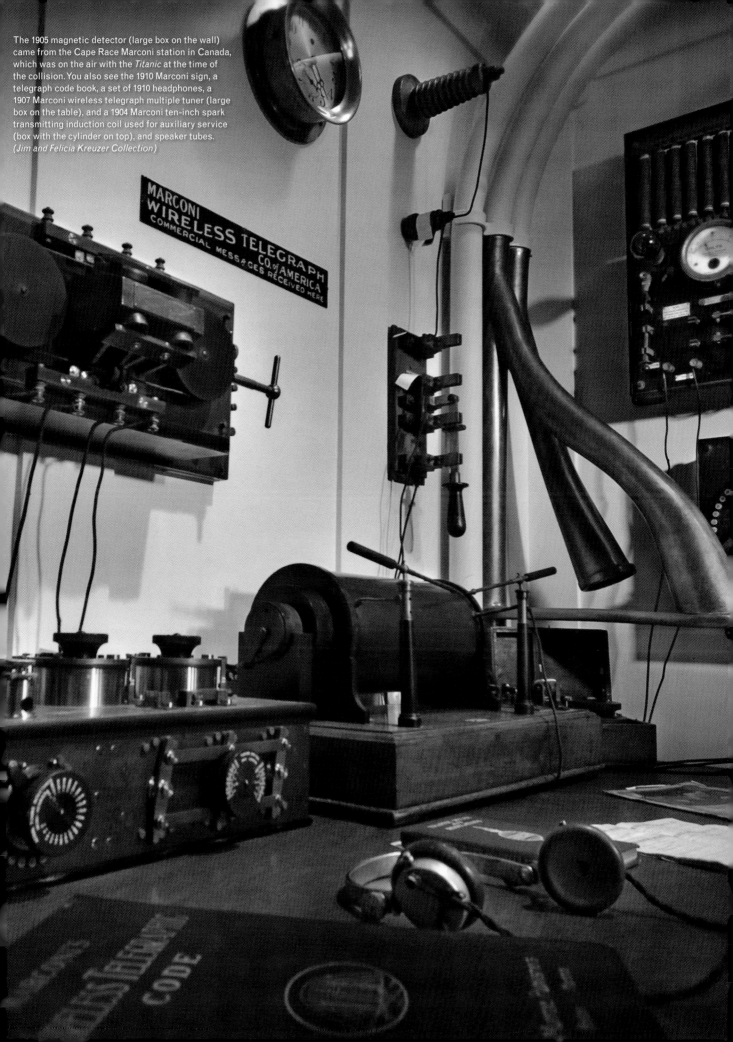

The 1905 magnetic detector (large box on the wall) came from the Cape Race Marconi station in Canada, which was on the air with the *Titanic* at the time of the collision. You also see the 1910 Marconi sign, a telegraph code book, a set of 1910 headphones, a 1907 Marconi wireless telegraph multiple tuner (large box on the table), and a 1904 Marconi ten-inch spark transmitting induction coil used for auxiliary service (box with the cylinder on top), and speaker tubes. *(Jim and Felicia Kreuzer Collection)*

They were responsible only to the captain, and the buttons of their uniforms sported the Marconi emblem.

The wireless room actually consisted of two rooms. The Silent Room was soundproofed, designed to house the transmitting equipment and shield both the operators and passengers from the electrical racket of generators, batteries, and crackling sparks. The more familiar Marconi Room, where crew or passengers could send or receive Marconigrams, was an office containing the operator's work station, spark telegraph keys, and receiving equipment. Adjacent to this office was a bedroom where the operators slept. Those who sat at the controls of the Marconi Wireless could never stray far from their post, as one never knew when contact with the outside world would become a necessity.

Such was the case on the night of April 14, 1912.

Shortly after the *Titanic*'s fatal collision, the Marconi operators took to their stations and began frantically to send out distress signals. The working range of the ship's wireless was said to be 250 miles; however, at night, due to atmospheric conditions, it was very possible to transmit a message two thousand miles or more. The motor generators whirred and charged up the batteries, an electrical spark leapt, and the air filled with the hot scent of ozone. The operators played their spark telegraph keys like concert pianists, over and over tapping the universally known distress signals, SOS and CQD.

It is said that the wireless operators, courageous and determined, stayed at their posts until the last moments. They struggled and fought to send a message to anyone who might hear, who could possibly offer help. Their frustration must have been unfathomable as water filled the boiler room and took out their main power source. Undaunted, they switched to battery power and continued to transmit. When battery power was depleted, a standby spark transmitter was put into operation. It would eventually fall silent as well.

But the men from Marconi had achieved their goal; the message had been heard. The *Carpathia*, about fifty miles away, began steaming toward the *Titanic* at full speed, dodging fields of icebergs and putting both herself and her crew in grave danger. She would arrive in time to save the 712 passengers and crewmen who had escaped to the lifeboats but too late to help the almost fifteen hundred who had lost their lives to the sea.

The waters of the Atlantic were at twenty-eight degrees Fahrenheit in the early hours of April 15, 1912. Those in the lifeboats were freezing, most without heavy jackets, hats, or gloves. Because of the speed at which the disaster occurred, with no time for planning, the lifeboats held virtually no provisions. If not for the arrival of the *Carpathia,* the 712 survivors would have endured a slow and nightmarish demise, rowing slowly into an icy eternity. If not for the miracle of Marconi's amazing wireless, *Carpathia* would not have come.

The most historically accurate recreation of the *Titanic* wireless room using authentic Marconi equipment is at the museum in Branson. It was reconstructed using photographs of the wireless room of the *Olympic* and Father Browne's photograph of the *Titanic* wireless room. The Marconi telegraph and the distress signal it sent, which was heard by the *Carpathia*, can be credited with the saving of 712 souls. *(Jim and Felicia Kreuzer Collection)*

These replicas model precisely the highly polished brass telegraphs which relayed directions to the engine rooms, the sturdy steering stand with its Brown's Patent Telemotor Wheel. Four priceless ship's compasses were the pride of the *Titanic* bridge. In 1912, this command center of the liner was considered state-of-the-art.

THE BRIDGE

THE WINDOWS TO THE STARS SPANNED THE SHIP

Captain Edward Smith relaxed in his spacious stateroom. The hour was late. His ship's clock chimed 11:30 PM, and he looked forward to a good night's sleep. At age sixty-two, Edward had accomplished great things in his life. Born an only child in Hanley-Stoke, England, he had traveled to Liverpool at the age of thirteen to find work on the sea. After seventeen years spent learning all he could of the seaman's life, he joined the White Star Line in 1880. Less than a decade later, by his thirty-seventh birthday, Edward had taken command of his first ship. Since 1904, he had acted as Commodore of the entire White Star fleet.

By title, Edward was captain of the *Olympic, Titanic's* sister ship. However, by policy, he always sailed White Star's newest vessels on their maiden voyage. His presence on these journeys was required not just out of tradition but also out of morale and matters of customer service. Edward was not just competent in his job and knowledgeable of the sea, he was also a man of cheerful spirits. The other ship's officers held him in high esteem, but more importantly, the wealthy passengers who provided much of White Star's high profits were enamored with the man. It was not unheard of for the socially elite to postpone passage on a vessel unless Captain Smith was at the helm.

And, this was his final transatlantic crossing as master of a luxury liner. After more than thirty years spent in the employment of the White Star Line — twenty-five of them as captain — it was time for the old sailor to come home from the sea. He sought to return to England and to enjoy the comforts of home with his wife, Eleanor, and Melville, the daughter who was born shortly after his forty-eighth birthday.

It was now 11:35 PM. On the bridge of the *Titanic,* First Officer William Murdoch was standing his watch as the duty officer. At age thirty-nine, he realized that his future was as bright as Edward's had been at the same age. Here he was, third in command on the pride of the White Star fleet.

For the time being, high in the superstructure of *Titanic,* he was in charge of the ship's command center with its state-of-the-art equipment. Spanning the width of the ship, the bridge was open on the sides but protected by glass windows in front. Bridges were so named because, originally, they were simple catwalks that allowed a commanding officer to view his ship's sides while docking. It was only about 1900 that glass windows had begun to be installed on bridges to offer protection from wind and rain.

From the bridge, William peered into the cold night. He would have noticed the gleaming brass of the telegraphs, the devices that relayed orders such as "full," "ahead," "dead slow," and "stop," to the engine rooms. He stood near the steering stand, with its majestic wheel that was used for steering during fair weather and while

entering and exiting ports, and glanced at the ship's compass to assure that all coordinates were correct. The *Titanic*, unlike most ships, had four of these priceless compasses, encased in protective binnacles.

He possibly considered the helmsman, who was presently controlling the ship's steering from a heated wheelhouse behind the bridge. In that small structure was not only the main steering wheel and a compass but also an array of telephones that were connected to integral stations around the liner.

One of these phones was in the crow's nest. Suddenly, William heard the ringing of the ship's bell. Immediately after, one of the bridge phones began to ring. The sixth officer, twenty-four-year-old James Moody, grabbed the receiver and relayed the message to William. Crewman Frederick Fleet had spotted an iceberg — and it was dead ahead!

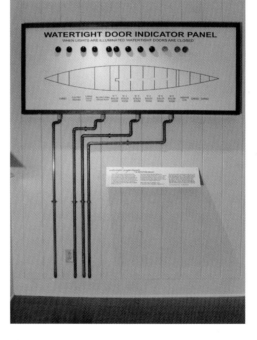

William, quick in both feet and thoughts, ordered a turn to hard starboard in a desperate attempt to avoid disaster. *Titanic* responded, and if she'd had but a few more seconds, she might well have missed the berg entirely. The bow swung twenty-two degrees in thirty-seven seconds, enough to avoid a head-on collision but not enough to escape the fatal wounds ripped into her steel-plated sides.

The captain was already out of his cabin and rushing toward the wheelhouse. He ordered his fourth officer, twenty-eight-year-old Joseph Groves Boxhall, to inspect the ship for damage. Upon hearing Groves's terrifying report, Edward knew the truth.

The time was 12:05 AM. Edward instructed his chief officer, thirty-nine-year-old Henry Wilde, to begin uncovering the lifeboats. At 12:10 AM, he told First Wireless Operator Jack Phillips to begin sending out the distress call.

Most of the *Titanic's* other officers, thirty-eight-year-old Second Officer Charles Lightoller, thirty-four-year-old Third Officer Herbert John Pitman, and twenty-nine-year-old Fifth Officer Harold Lowe, had already retired for the night. All would throw on uniforms, pull on boots, and dash to the bridge. Within moments of arrival, they would jump into action.

William Murdoch had already closed the watertight doors in the boiler and engine rooms. Next, he ordered Herbert Pitman to the boat deck to assist in loading passengers. Within two hours, Pitman would be placed in charge of Lifeboat Number 5. He wished to return to the scene of the disaster and search for survivors, but he was unable to do so after facing a revolt from passengers who were afraid those in the water would swamp the small boat.

Joseph Boxhall fired the first of the distress rockets and made his way to the boat deck. After helping women and children into Lifeboat Number 2, he would take his place in the small craft and direct the freezing passengers to row away from the *Titanic* with all their might. He would also live, but, like Herbert, was persuaded by passengers not to return to look for those who still might survive in the frigid waters.

James Moody did his part in loading passengers, and when all boats were gone, he attempted to launch a collapsible survival raft. He was never seen again.

Harold Lowe, commanding Lifeboat Number 4, wisely off-loaded the passengers he tended into other lifeboats. Bravely, he returned to *Titanic* in search of survivors. He found but four, only three of whom would survive.

Frederick Fleet, who had spotted the iceberg from the crow's nest, was able to find a haven in Lifeboat Number 6.

Telegraph operator Jack Phillips stayed at his post, as did his fellow operator Harold Bride, until being released by the captain. With power gone, the decks at a severe angle, and waters rising, both dove into the twenty-eight-degree water. Miraculously, they spotted the overturned hull of one of the collapsible rafts and climbed aboard. They would hold onto the tiny raft for hours. Bride would survive, but Phillips would perish sometime before dawn.

Henry Wilde and William Murdoch would meet their doom on the morning of April 15; their bodies were never recovered.

And as for Captain Edward Smith, the grizzled veteran would obey without question the unwritten bylaw of ship's masters from time immemorial.

He went down with the ship.

A young visitor to the *Titanic* Museum in Branson leans on an authentic reproduction of the ship's railing, perhaps pondering the mysteries of the universe. It is entirely possible that, on the night of April 14, 1912, another young man stared into the night sky before feeling the shudder from impact with the iceberg that would sink the ship.

THE LONGEST THREE HOURS OF THEIR LIVES

It is often said that, when faced with ominous danger, one's life will flash before one's eyes. Within the space of mere seconds, a person confronting his or her own demise will witness past, present, and future. That person will recall passions, fears, great loves, and loves unrequited. The canvas of the mind will be painted with the joys, the pains, the laughter, the tears — all that brought them to the edge of the abyss.

On April 14 and 15, 1912, between the hours of 11:40 PM and 2:20 AM, this was the burden borne by those who sailed on the *Titanic*. However, another impression, equally as daunting, was at play. While thoughts of their existence thrust themselves to the forefront of the passengers' perceptions, time slowed to a crawl. There are occurrences when the entirety of our beings seems to pass in a heartbeat. On the same token, when fear looms large, the terror of the inevitable can make minutes seem like hours and hours like days.

For three hours, they waited. For three hours, they prayed. For three hours, they hoped against hope that a miracle would rescue them from the cold, cold grasp of death. This was but one of the curses that lay at the feet of those who sailed upon the *Titanic*.

It was 11:40 PM when Frederick Fleet and Reginald Lee, manning the crow's nest fifty feet above the *Titanic*'s deck, saw the shadow loom on the horizon. Their work shift would have ended in twenty minutes, and as they viewed the calm seas and starry night, their thoughts were of a warm bed and a good night's sleep.

Spotting the massive berg grow in the distance, those thoughts became like smoke on the breeze. Frederick rang the bell three times, grabbed the crow's nest phone and called the bridge. When Officer James Moody answered, he heard only the words, "Iceberg right ahead!"

Less than a minute after that first sighting, *Titanic* collided with the berg. By 11:50 PM, the ship's six watertight compartments had overflowed. The ship's post office on G deck forward was two-feet deep in frigid water. The postal clerks, holding true to the mantra of those who truly believe "the mail must go through," began transferring bags to the boat decks for loading in the lifeboats.

Midnight came, and after an inspection of the damage, the managing director of Harland and Wolff gave a grim report. If anyone knew the *Titanic*, it was Thomas Andrews, and he explained to Captain Edward Smith that the unthinkable had happened to the unsinkable. *Titanic* had but two, maybe three hours, before she sank to the ocean floor.

Immediately, the captain ordered First Officer Henry Wilde and Second Officer Charles Lightoller to ready the lifeboats. Wireless operator Jack Phillips sent out the CQD distress call, "We've struck an iceberg." The message and the ship's position were received by wireless operators in Cape Race, Newfoundland.

The clock ticked, and at 12:25 AM, the wireless operator on the *Carpathia*, Harold Cottam, also received a message. "Come at once," it said. "We have struck an iceberg." *Carpathia*'s captain, Arthur Rostrum, had been on course for the Mediterranean and was transporting 743 passengers. Now committed to a rescue, he calculated distance and reckoned that the *Titanic* was fifty-eight miles away. He ordered a course change and called for full speed. Though a near impossible feat, the firemen on the *Carpathia* shoveled with all their might and increased the ship's speed from 12.5 to 17.5 knots.

At 12:45 AM, *Titanic*'s first starboard lifeboat was lowered into the water. Sadly, it held barely half its capacity of sixty-four passengers. Those on deck watched the skies. At intervals of every five to ten minutes, the heavens would come ablaze as the *Titanic* crew launched distress rockets. The loading of the boats continued with

Within just seven to nine minutes of breaking into two major pieces, the *Titanic* would land on the ocean floor. The bow landed first, still upright, and the hull sank into the mud floor of the ocean. The stern landed two minutes later about one-third of a mile away. Within one-half hour, passengers who had not drowned would succumb to hypothermia.

few occupied to maximum. By 1:30 AM, the last lifeboat on the starboard side was lowered, and shortly after, *Carpathia* heard a final, weak signal from the *Titanic*: "Engine room is full to the boilers." Twenty minutes later, the last lifeboat on the port side was launched. Those who remained aboard the massive liner could do little but wait for the end.

Several collapsible lifeboats did remain on the deck, and White Star Line President J. Bruce Ismay sneaked into one of these, forever earning him the slur, "J. Brute Ismay." It was put into the water only two-thirds full. Another collapsible was located, and it entered the water bearing only thirty-three passengers. Escape was now impossible for the fifteen hundred souls who remained aboard, and as water poured over the forward section of the *Titanic* and the bow began to sink, the masses raced toward the rising stern.

At 2:18 AM, the lights flickered and died. *Titanic* split into two pieces between the third and fourth funnels. The stern, which had slanted upward at a severe angle, crashed back into the Atlantic. Filling with water, it began to rise at a breakneck pace as the bow sheared off completely. Within two minutes, the remains of the *Titanic* were making a final journey toward the ocean floor, over twelve thousand feet below.

Floundering in the twenty-eight degree water, fifty passengers spotted two damaged collapsibles. Twenty survivors held tightly to the partially submerged Collapsible A while thirty more clambered atop the overturned Collapsible B.

For the rest of the *Titanic*'s ill-fated voyagers, death would come at a snail's pace, by drowning or hypothermia. Shortly after hitting the water, they became numb and short of breath. Within five minutes they were unable to control their shivering, and the core temperatures of their bodies dropped to dangerous levels. All thought was gone; the ability to speak was absent. The only instinct remaining was that of animal survival. Half an hour would pass before most of these poor unfortunates would succumb to hypothermia.

Some of the lifeboats returned to look for survivors. Fourteen people, still grasping Collapsible A, were pulled from the brine. Possibly as many as thirty men were rescued from Collapsible B. Finally, at 4 AM, the *Carpathia* arrived on the scene. For the next four hours, lifeboats straggled toward the safety of the liner, their angel of mercy. By 6:30 AM, Bruce Ismay arrived. At 8:30 AM, the lifeboat captained by officer Charles Lightoller made its way to *Carpathia*'s hull. Charles would remain on the small boat until all his charges were safely aboard. He would be the final survivor to leave a lifeboat.

The *Carpathia* steamed back toward New York and arrived on Thursday, April 18, 1912. For some, life had been snuffed out like a sputtering candle. For others, lost and wandering in the lifeboats, the fear of perishing at sea had played out for an eternity.

For all those who survived, the memory would burn till their dying day.

Under Pressure

The *Titanic* rests at a depth of more than twelve thousand feet. How deep is that? The maximum depth that can be obtained by a U.S. Navy Seawolf submarine is two thousand feet. At one mile below the ocean's surface, sea creatures become semi-transparent and/or have bioluminescent organs. At two miles, the water temperature hovers just above the freezing point.

Distance or oxygen itself is not the problem; it is the pressure. Water pressure exerted at these depths will crush most anything not specifically designed to live there. Only the most technologically advanced devices, constructed of space-age materials and tested again and again, can handle the pressure of the ocean. Anything less would be crushed as easily as a foam cup.

This is how the *Titanic* lies today. The bow sank almost intact, while eighteen hundred feet away, the stern lies mangled, the poop deck flattened. As the bow sank, the air inside was slowly replaced by water, allowing it to retain its shape. The stern became more compressed the deeper it plunged, because air in its enclosed areas did not escape. When the pressure inside exceeded the pressure exerted from the outside water, the stern imploded.

INTERACTIVE GALLERY

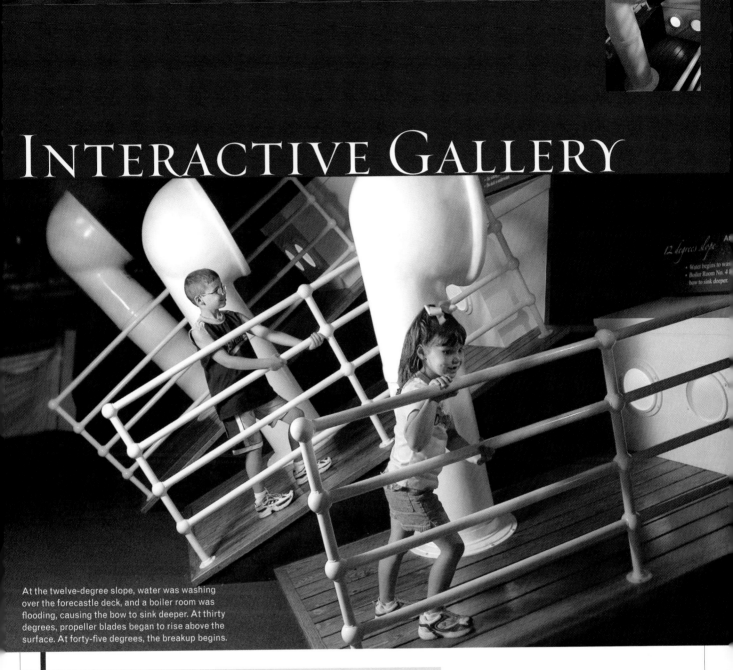

At the twelve-degree slope, water was washing over the forecastle deck, and a boiler room was flooding, causing the bow to sink deeper. At thirty degrees, propeller blades began to rise above the surface. At forty-five degrees, the breakup begins.

WHERE THE EXPERIENCE BECOMES REAL

The ancient Greeks knew all about hubris, the tendency to engage in exhibitions of excessive pride, arrogance, or a lack of humility. It was their belief that such behavior would result in extreme punishment from the gods, and being a creative bunch, they expected supernatural retribution via being turned into a rock, a spider, or having their liver pecked on for eternity by a disgruntled eagle.

Yes, the ancient Greeks knew all about hubris. Unfortunately, the designers, crew, and many passengers aboard the *Titanic* did not. Technology appeared at a breakneck pace in the Edwardian age, and by the time *Titanic*

left the Harland and Wolff shipyards, virtually the whole world believed she was unsinkable. Perhaps it's an inescapable human folly that mere mortals repeatedly attempt to assert supremacy over the forces of nature and the whims of fate.

The White Star Line owners promoted the *Titanic* as "practically unsinkable." Only twenty lifeboats were placed aboard. These consisted of fourteen wooden lifeboats, each thirty-feet long by nine-feet wide by four-feet deep and capable of holding sixty-five passengers; two rescue cutters of the same size as the wooden lifeboats, capable of carrying forty passengers each; and four collapsible lifeboats, twenty-seven-feet long, eight-feet wide and three-feet deep, each with room for forty-seven people.

These lifeboats were sturdy vessels, for as with all else on the *Titanic*, no expense was spared on quality. The boats were built with overlapping panels of pine, double fastened with copper nails and clinched-over roves. The keels were made of elm, the sterns of oak. The lifeboats were fabricated to withstand harsh conditions. Each came complete with oars, blankets, flares, and some basic provisions. The *Titanic* had the finest lifeboats money could buy.

Unfortunately, in the wee hours of April 14 and 15, 1912, quantity was a far more important consideration than quality.

Titanic carried, at best, only half the lifeboats needed for successful evacuation. If each boat had been filled to the maximum, 1,178 passengers could have been saved. On a ship carrying 2,208 passengers and crew, such is shoddy math. Granted, there were 3,560 cork-filled life jackets aboard, but glorified water-wings are of little use when floundering around in twenty-eight-degree water.

Still, one question has always remained a mystery. If the lifeboats could have taken nearly 1,200 passengers off the doomed ship, why were there only 712 survivors? The answer revolves around that one simple word: hubris.

Remember, the *Titanic* was deemed unsinkable. The year 1912 was a simpler time than now, and such claims arising from a respected firm such as White Star Line were taken as gospel.

Plus, at least among the wealthy, this likely was not their first ocean voyage. They felt secure.

It is also a fact that, in the first hour or so after *Titanic* collided with the iceberg, many passengers refused to believe the obvious. Even though the crew tried to explain and pleaded the necessity of boarding the lifeboats before they were sent away, many voyagers wholly rejected the news that *Titanic*'s fate was sealed. The lights were still burning on the giant liner, the heat was still on, and the cabins were warm. The word for the day was denial. Even many women with children in tow preferred to remain on the "unsinkable" ship rather than face the dangers of floating in the Atlantic in an oversized rowboat.

There were other reasons why so many of the boats were filled to only half capacity. Some people became lost in the maze of corridors that comprised the massive ship; others tried to pull trunks and luggage down the passageways. A few accepted their fate, believing in "women and children first" and either engaged in prayer, assisted in the loading, or headed for the closest available liquor cabinet.

Some women chose to remain with their husbands, and the ship stewardess or matron, Sarah Stap, age forty-seven, offered her seat to a young cabin boy, proclaiming she had lived her life.

The crew did the only thing possible. They loaded the first boats with as many passengers as would enter and lowered them into the water as quickly as possible.

One who did not believe the *Titanic* could sink was fifty-two-year-old Major Arthur Godfrey Peuchen. Born in Montreal, Quebec, and president of the Standard Chemical Company, Peuchen was on his way home to Toronto, Ontario. When told by a steward that the ship had hit an iceberg and was sinking,

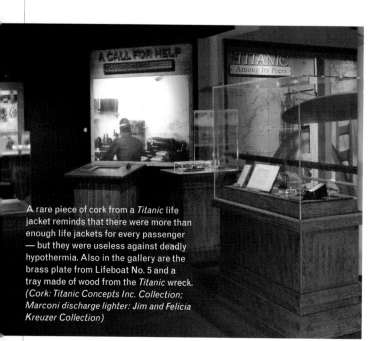

A rare piece of cork from a *Titanic* life jacket reminds that there were more than enough life jackets for every passenger — but they were useless against deadly hypothermia. Also in the gallery are the brass plate from Lifeboat No. 5 and a tray made of wood from the *Titanic* wreck. *(Cork: Titanic Concepts Inc. Collection; Marconi discharge lighter: Jim and Felicia Kreuzer Collection)*

How Cold Was It?

The water temperature was a freezing 28F degrees (-2.2C) when the *Titanic* went down.

Most passengers and crew struggling to stay afloat in the water succumbed to hypothermia within 20 minutes.

The normal human body temperature is 98.6F degrees (37C). If it falls below 95F degrees (35C) hypothermia sets in.

The first symptom of hypothermia is shivering, which gradually lessens as the body's temperature drops. Victims' pulses become slow and weak, and their breathing becomes shallow. Then, they grow very sleepy and confused and may suffer from hallucinations before finally losing consciousness.

TIME HOW LONG YOU CAN KEEP YOUR FINGER IN THE WATER!

PRESS TO START
PRESS TO STOP

Margaret Brown
AGE: 44
FIRST CLASS PASSENGER

Margaret has a few words with Robert Hichens...

LIFEBOAT FACTS

The exterior was built with overlapping planks of yellow pine, double-fastened with copper nails and clinched over roves (small, slightly convex rings of copper placed over boat nails)...

Visitors can sit in the full-scale replica of Lifeboat No. 6, and feel the pain of twenty-eight degree water. Designed to hold sixty-five passengers but lowered with only twenty-four, Lifeboat No. 6 was commanded by the dour Cornishman Robert Hichens. Margaret Brown, who later became known as "The Unsinkable Molly Brown" fought with him, even threatening to throw him overboard, for refusing to go back to seek survivors. *(Molly Brown Photo: Randy Bryan Bigham Collection)*

LIVERPOOL

30'-0
9'-6 X 4'-6

A full-scale replica of Lifeboat No. 6, which departed only half-full.

he simply took the dire prognosis as the ramblings of a nervous crewman. Finally, playing the odds, he did venture up to the boat deck. He took with him only three oranges for a snack and a tiny pearl pin. In his cabin, he left two hundred thousand dollars in stock and bond certificates and a treasure in personal jewelry.

Peuchen came to his senses before it was too late, and because he was a yachtsman, was asked to help crew Lifeboat Number 6. He survived the disaster, although in retrospect

The museum contains six original newspapers published the day after or within a few days of the sinking, including newspapers from New York and Washington. *(This newspaper: Titanic Concepts Inc. Collection)*

his two hundred thousand dollars would have undoubtedly given him more pleasure than his trio of citrus snacks.

The lifeboats were long gone by 1:50 AM on the morning of April 15, 1912, and those left aboard *Titanic* almost assuredly knew that the end was near. The deck was now at a twelve-degree slope, and anything not nailed down was beginning to slide. By 2:05 AM, all doubts of "unsinkable" had fled, as the deck was at a thirty-degree slope and awash with seawater.

At 2:18 AM, the propellers began to rise out of the water. The deck tilted forty-five degrees, and only those holding on for dear life were prevented from sliding the length of the ship and being battered, pummeled, or crushed by equipment and furniture in total free-fall. The ship splits into two pieces between the third and fourth funnel. The bow begins to sink, and a section of the stern falls back into the water, rises, and then begins to fill with water and sink. Two minutes later, the *Titanic* was no more.

Hubris had once again collected her due.

NOON EDITION
NOON EDITION
ROCHESTER EVENING TIMES

GREAT DEMAND THAT LOSS OF 1,500 SOULS BE AVENGED

TWO CONTINENTS UNITE IN EFFORT TO PUNISH GUILTY

SURVIVORS ON CARPATHIA'S DECKS

ROCHESTER GIRL ON HONOR ROLL OF TITANIC HEROINES

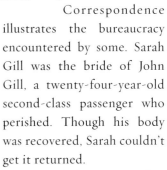

DISCOVERY GALLERY

THE AFTERMATH OF THE TRAGEDY

The mind is literally stunned by the historical memorabilia in this gallery. Documenting the aftermath of the tragedy are letters from survivors describing the ghastly ordeal of watching the breakup of the ship and listening to fellow passengers drown, correspondence from survivors seeking remuneration, photographs of lifeboats approaching the rescue ship *Carpathia*, and photographs of salvage crews performing the grisly task of recovering bodies.

For instance, the death certificate of thirty-five-year-old John Boyd, a first-class steward on the *Titanic*, is at first glance simply a record of his demise — until you learn his body was never recovered. Hundreds of bodies were not found, intensifying the grief of families who would never again see their loved ones.

By the same token, on display are designations of heroism given to those who fought their fears and placed themselves in peril to save others.

A silver loving cup, presented to Captain Arthur Rostron of the *Carpathia* by Margaret "The Unsinkable Molly" Brown, portrays her profound gratitude. The captain had taken the *Carpathia* at high speeds through iceberg laden waters, risking the same fate as *Titanic*, and if not for his bravery, all of the *Titanic's* passengers might well have been lost. Captain Rostron was later a guest of President William Howard Taft and was awarded the Congressional Gold Medal, the highest civilian honor that can be bestowed by the U.S. Congress. Medals were also presented by survivors to the officers and crew of the RMS *Carpathia*.

Relief fund checks show the outpouring of heartfelt desire by ordinary people to help survivors.

Correspondence illustrates the bureaucracy encountered by some. Sarah Gill was the bride of John Gill, a twenty-four-year-old second-class passenger who perished. Though his body was recovered, Sarah couldn't get it returned.

She did receive her husband's possessions. They arrived, packaged in a simple brown envelope. Included was a canvas bag for personal belongings, a pocket comb, pocketbook, gold watch and chain, silver matchbox, keys, pocketknife, collar button and $47.60 in silver coins and notes.

However, as heartless as it seems, the company informed her that she would have to pay twenty English pounds (roughly fourteen hundred dollars at

Lady Duff Gordon gave her self-inscribed photo to Carpathia passenger Dr. Frank Blackmarr for his assistance on the rescue ship. All classes on White Star Line ships were served on elegant china. This silver-plated cigarette case was a gift to survivor Henry Harper for his assistance to the widow of victim Howard Case. (Photo: Craig Sopin Collection; plate and cigarette case: Cedar Bay Entertainment Collection)

the time) or her husband's body would "regrettably" be buried at sea near Halifax. The shipping line informed Sarah that "the sinking was an unfortunate accident, for which we cannot be held responsible. We regret that we do not see our way to bring home the bodies of those recovered free of expense."

Sarah did not have the money to bring back the remains of her beloved, and true to their word, the White Star Line buried John Gill at sea on April 24, 1912. The already distraught Sarah was literally struck mute. Unable to speak for twenty years, she never remarried and used a bosun's whistle to communicate. In 1932, Sarah Gill fell down a flight of stairs, and her voice miraculously returned.

Why She Sank

The *Titanic* and her sister ship *Olympic* were the first ships to contain watertight bulkheads below the decks. There were sealed tanks in the double-bottomed hull, with the lower hull being divided into sixteen watertight compartments. The ship would not sink if any two amidships compartments, such as the engine or boiler room, were breached, or if the first four compartments were to flood. But the design had several flaws, one being that the decks themselves weren't watertight due to staircases, ladders, and elevators. Plus, the bulkheads did not extend above D Deck. In other words, if the bow of the ship was to flood, the weight of the water would pull it downward. Eventually, with nowhere else to go, the incoming water would rise up through the decks, overflow the bulkheads, and spill into the remaining compartments.

That is exactly what happened.

Continuing
The
Legend...

The Discovery Gallery is a treasury of photographs and artifacts from the *Titanic* or its passengers, including the White Star Line letter to Sarah Gill. A Ken Marschall reproduction provides a backdrop for the gallery. The deck chair was salvaged by a Canadian fisheries vessel, then tacked onto a church wall in Quebec as a tribute to victims, next stored in a Quebec barn, and finally rediscovered in the 1990s. *(Letter: Stan Lehrer Collection; deck chair: Titanic Concepts Inc. Collection; painting: Courtesy of Ken Marschall.)*

The *Titanic* tragedy has long been a target for movies, from a quickly released short and purportedly documentary film in 1912 through many others, including one named simply *Titanic* and noted for accuracy in details in 1953, starring Barbara Stanwyck, Clifton Wells, and Robert Wagner, and another, the memorable 1958 *A Night to Remember*.

But it is only the latest, James Cameron's 1997 Academy Award-winning *Titanic* starring Leonardo DiCaprio and Kate Winslet, that let millions of viewers see the great ship as she is underwater today during the telling of the epic tale.

The movie starts with an eerie scene two-and-a-half miles below the North Atlantic. To make that scene, Director James Cameron built this twenty-six-foot model, based on film footage captured by underwater cameras used by the discoverer and other explorers of the wreck. This model, a masterpiece of design and detail, accurately portrays how the *Titanic* appears today, buried in the mud at the bottom of the sea. It had never been available for viewing until placed in this gallery.

MEMORIAL ROOM

HOW WE REMEMBER AND WHY WE REMEMBER

It is difficult to imagine the impact that the sinking of the *Titanic* had upon the world of 1912. Wireless telegraphy, as pioneered by Marconi, was still in its infancy. The first actual radio news program was not broadcast until August 31, 1920, and radio as a source of news and entertainment would not become popular until well into the 1920s.

Today, we live in a world of instant and constant communication. We hear of disasters moments after they occur, sometimes as they are happening. While humanity is neither heartless nor lacking in compassion, the mass media's ability to inundate the globe with reports of tragedy after tragedy has led us to become desensitized to all but the most horrendous of disasters.

Nearly a century ago, the sinking of the *Titanic*, reported primarily by newspapers and word of mouth, shocked the planet into a state of collective mourning. The very idea of the deaths of 1,496 people aboard a ship that was considered the pinnacle of safety and technology was cause for alarm.

Around the world, people grieved. Memorials to those who had lost their lives sprang up at a frantic pace. The first Requiem Mass was held in St. Colman's Cathedral, in Queenstown, Ireland, on April 22, 1912. Bishop Robert

SYMBOLS OF SURVIVAL AND DEATH

The life jacket worn by eighteen-year-old Madeleine Astor, the pregnant bride of wealthy John Jacob Astor, is the only one in the world that can be linked to an individual. The watch was retrieved from an unidentified body, it's hands frozen in time fifteen minutes after the ship sank. *(Life jacket: Titanic Historical Society/Ed and Karen Kamuda Collection; watch: Cedar Bay Entertainment Collection)*

Browne was presiding. He knew how close he had come to losing his beloved nephew, Father Francis Browne, whose photographic records provided the very last pictures of the *Titanic* and her passengers. What if the Bishop had purchased a ticket that took his nephew all the way to America? Father Francis himself had expressed a desire to remain onboard beyond Queenstown.

On November 4, 1912, a carved plaque, dedicated to the *Titanic's* eight members of the band, was placed at the Liverpool Philharmonic Hall. This plaque survived the burning of the hall in 1933 and was reinstalled six years later at the new home of the Liverpool Philharmonic. Both the new hall and the plaque survived bombings during World War II.

The body of the *Titanic's* bandleader, Wallace Hartley, was recovered two weeks after the sinking. It is said he was still in his band uniform, his violin strapped to his body. Hartley's corpse was transported to Liverpool and then taken sixty miles by horse-drawn hearse to his hometown of Colne. Over thirty thousand people lined the route to pay their respects. A marble memorial to Hartley resides just off the main street which enters Colne; to this day he is regarded as the town's greatest hero.

On April 15, 1913, the *Titanic* Memorial Lighthouse, at that time sitting atop the Seaman's Church Institute, was dedicated in New York. Today, the lighthouse can be found at the South Street Seaport Museum in New York.

The Women's *Titanic* Memorial was originally erected in 1933 in Washington D.C.'s Rock Creek Park. President Herbert Hoover and the wife of former President William H. Taft attended the unveiling. Today it is located close to Fort McNair.

The list goes on and on. A life-size bronze statue of *Titanic* Captain Edward Smith can be found in Beacon Park, Lichfield, England. Soon after it was reported that he had drowned with the rest, a memorial was planned for Major Archibald Butt of Augusta, Georgia. Today, visitors to Augusta continue to travel across the illuminated, Archibald Butt Memorial Bridge.

Remembrances of this type can be found all over the globe, but the most recent is certainly the Memorial Room found in the *Titanic* Museum in Branson, Missouri. Each passenger was lovingly researched by Phillip Gowan, who obtained copies of birth and death certificates for almost every passenger. For the first time, ages of each passenger were verified, and Phillip has written a brief story, itself a kind of memorial, about each passenger. The stories are printed on boarding passes handed to visitors as they enter the museum.

Intended as a place of reverence and dedicated to the memory of all who were aboard, the Memorial Room features four illuminated glass panels etched with the names of all who sailed on the *Titanic*. Their status as survivors or victims is signified by a simple underscoring of survivors' names.

While it may be true that we of the modern age have become somewhat desensitized to misfortune and calamity, the story of the *Titanic* somehow surpasses our tendency to forget or ignore.

The *Titanic* is timeless.